Margot
47574

As told by
Sharma L. Wolff
and
Carol L. Miller, Ph.D.

Acknowledgements

We would like to thank the following friends and family members for their assistance and encouragement: Cyrus Wolff, Elias Wolff, Timothy Wolff, Robert Miller, Rose Nolen, Lorraine Tressel (who introduced us to Margot), Shary Potter, photographer Dani Steele and Quantico Book Club Readers: Trina Nolen, Jess Moen, Carol Peterson, Sylvia Baufield, Cindy Gillette and Laurene Wenstrand. We would also like to acknowledge the Jewish Community Relations Council of Minnesota and the Dakotas. It is the program that runs the speakers Bureau; Tolerance Minnesota.

Dedication

This book is dedicated to Margot's audiences - those who have listened and learned over the years. Many have shared with Margot that hearing her story has changed their lives, and has therefore given her life purpose.

To order additional copies of this book, please send an email to: margot47574@yahoo.com or call Carol Miller at 763-577-0729

Printed by Pressworks, Inc.
Plymouth, MN, USA

Margot
47574

Table of Contents

Carol's Foreword

Are there enough stories of holocaust survivors?
No. As recently as last month, I read a claim that the
holocaust was "exaggerated beyond belief." It takes every
survivor's account to testify against the World War II
lunacy. It also takes historians, sociologists, clergymen,
educators, soldiers, politicians, farmers, physicians,
journalists, authors, families and other citizens of the
world. It takes scrapbooks, letters, photographs, diaries and
official documents. World War II should be required study
in schools. We must never let the subject be neglected.
We owe this to millions of Jews, millions of nomads,
homosexuals, and other Nazi victims. We also owe allied
soldiers, civilian Resistance workers, military prisoners of
war and volunteers who staffed hospitals and humanitarian
organizations in the united opposition to the Third Reich.
(My family sent six men and one woman into the WWII
military, including my father.)

Now you have the opportunity to read the unique
account of Ruth Margot DeWilde in <u>Margot 47574</u>.
Hers are important true stories of man's inhumanity and
Margot's personal victory. You will read about a woman
who always had hope and an inner fire and who refused
to cooperate with the Nazis – by seeming to cooperate.
Although the affects of war are far-reaching and long-
lasting, victims can change as they have time to ponder
and continue their journeys. With luck and determination,
Margot has lived beyond the horrors of World War II. She
emerged with a unique philosophy.

Margot DeWilde and Sharma Wolff are fascinating
women. They represent the generations before and after

me. Margot is 47 years older than Sharma. They are curious, sensitive, hopeful, and smart people. Sharma has a life-long love of new, unique projects. She is not afraid of deep water. Her ability to organize and her artistic bent make her capable of this job. To write Margot's story, they combined their attributes and experiences. Margot's years during World War II tap into Sharma's interest in history and her experience as an army veteran. Most profoundly, they respect all life.

I am Margot's friend and Sharma's mother. Margot is a role model. I wonder if I could face such a horrendous situation with courage. She continuously tells us that her experience, although collective on one level, is also her unique story.

To say that there is a Margot-Sharma bond is an understatement. Because of Margot's Auschwitz experience, she was not able to be a mother. The reader will learn about Margot's parents, brother and husbands. It has been a privilege to participate in this writing collaboration. It goes beyond caring - all the way to double love.

The chapters were written in third-person because Margot did not like first-person. "That is too much about me and I," she said. We were, however, able to include a short question and answer section as a follow-up to each chapter. This lets the reader hear Margot's own voice. Each chapter ends with letters from school children. The letters were selected from hundreds of notes Margot received and treasures. Sharma designed the book cover as a special tribute and gift to Margot.

Carol L. Miller, Ph.D.
Plymouth, Minnesota

Sharma's Foreword

I first met Margot when I heard her give a talk at a meeting of the Philolectian Society in Osseo, Minnesota. She calmly and unemotionally told of her experiences as a subject in the horrific medical experiments of Joseph Mengele. I was fascinated by her bravery in keeping hopeful and resolved through years of imprisonment in Auschwitz, near starvation, and the ever-present threat of death.

After Margot's talk, I began to examine life and view things differently. I did not realize how differently, though, until a couple weeks later when I was having a hard time accomplishing a daily chore. I was being thwarted and began to lament to myself that this particular task always seemed so difficult. Then, at that moment, I thought of Margot and all that she had been through, and my life changed. I realized that what I was experiencing was nothing at all compared to what she had lived through. I have never been faced with the threat of death on a daily basis. That in itself is difficult to even imagine. I have never been subjected to the senseless and nefarious whims of others or suffered physical privations from lack of food or extended exposure to extreme cold. I realized that how I view my experiences in life is a matter of perspective and is completely within my control. And ever since then, I have used this tool. When things seem bleak or difficult or I feel down, I often think of Margot and it changes my perspective. It makes me look at things from a different angle, to not take so much for granted, to ponder all I have to be thankful for. This concept is not new, of course, but hearing Margot's story is what it took to incorporate it into my life.

Because of the shift in perspective that Margot brought about in me, I felt it was important to have her story written down so that she could continue to inspire others even after she is no longer able to speak in person to audiences. Therefore, I approached her with the idea of working together to write her story. I feel very fortunate that she accepted the offer and was willing to share so much with me. It has been my honor to work with Margot, alongside my mother, Carol Miller, to document her story in writing. I have learned a great deal from her and will always be grateful that she was willing to be so open and share her experiences with us.

Margot has inspired many people, as proven by the hundreds of letters she received throughout the years. I have read many stories of the Holocaust, but to actually meet someone in person who has been there and experienced what Margot has, is far different. It brings the story to life and makes it real. I think that is why she has been able to inspire so many with her talks. We included a brief question and answer section after each chapter, to give a more personal aspect of Margot. It is my hope that in some small way her written story will continue to live on and bring hope to others, as well.

One of the most amazing things about Margot is that she has progressed through life and all her ordeals without feeling sorry for herself. Rather, she has faced her experiences with courage and fortitude and an attitude of defiance toward her oppressors. The strength and perseverance she has shown is an important lesson of encouragement and revelation.

Sharma Wolff
Princeton, Minnesota

Prologue: Quiet Reflections

Margot 47574 is the memoir and testimony of Margot DeWilde, a survivor of the concentration camp at Auschwitz, Poland. Contained within these pages is the true story of her life. She has chosen to share her experiences with the world. Each concentration camp survivor has a personal story; no two are alike. The importance of documenting the histories before it is too late cannot be overstated.

Reflecting back on her life, Margot considers her most irrational act to be trying to make up for lost time after she was liberated. She thought she could do this after the war. She tried to erase from her mind what she had been through during the Holocaust, forget about the past, and enjoy herself. Margot wanted to experience life to its fullest. She wanted to compensate for the freedom that had been stolen.

Margot now feels she was very irresponsible during the years following the war. She made a lot of mistakes and disappointed many people. Margot thinks she could have done a better job; been more useful. After her liberation from Auschwitz, Margot did not talk of her experiences for many years. She wanted that part of her past to be buried forever. But those experiences affected who she was and marred her soul. She could not escape them, no matter how hard she tried to divert herself. They made her feel she was somehow different from other people. She had trouble accepting herself. She eventually realized she had to face her memories and try to find some kind of meaning and purpose in them, in order to heal her wounds and find peace.

Margot believes that as injured parts become whole again and scars fade, so does our emotional state try to repair itself. Superficial scars heal faster than scars of an operation. The wounds of our minds take an even longer time to recover, sometimes resulting in scar tissue and abnormalities which never fully heal. She found that it is much harder to repair what one cannot see, in comparison to visible injuries. But given enough time, most emotional and mental wounds will heal.

Many years have passed since her internment. Margot has had a chance to reflect on all that has changed in her life. More than twenty years after the war ended, she started to tell others about what she had experienced during the Holocaust. She realized that her personal story is part of World War II history. The public should learn as much as possible about what the survivors endured. She has been speaking at schools, clubs and groups since 1969. At first, it was very difficult for her to talk about her past. It has grown easier over the years, but can still be painful. She continues to share her story because so many listeners have told her that it influences their lives and thus makes the telling worthwhile.

Margot has read in the newspaper that there are groups of people who deny the Holocaust. She considers the goal of her remaining years to voice the truth more often. She tells people who might not believe the stories that she was there. She is a witness of the cruel and corrupt Nazi regime. In particular, she is living proof of the horror of the Auschwitz medical experimentation block supervised by Josef Mengele.

After over two years of witnessing the changes that had taken place in Holland under the Nazi occupation, Margot, her husband and his family were arrested in 1943 as they attempted to flee to Switzerland. They were taken in a crowded train to Auschwitz. There they witnessed the sorting of lives; the split-second decision of who would live and who would die that day. Margot was one of the few chosen for a fate other than immediate death. Then, through a series of chance circumstances, she survived and lived to tell others what she witnessed. Now, in her later years, she feels an urgency to do just that. When talking to children who have just learned about the Holocaust, she encourages them to ask questions, so they will learn more about the persecution of the Jewish people.

Margot believes that our lives nowadays are so diverse and full of many obligations and interests that we do not take enough time to ponder the past. Very often smells, sights, and resemblances of circumstances that occurred during the war years transfer her back in time. She thinks about her unique horror and realizes that her life's story must be recorded. Otherwise, all that she has endured lacks purpose. She has written short parts of it throughout the years. Now she feels the need to connect the pieces of her past into a cohesive document.

She believes that everything which happens in one's life has a reason. Nothing is without a connection with events before and after it. She also believes that our being on earth has a certain purpose. Once we fulfill this purpose, we can leave in peace. In the recent past, Margot has had to confront the fact that her time might be running out. She sometimes wonders, "Has my procrastination to cohesively document my story been subconsciously a way to gain time? Am I really ready?"

As Margot recently stared at a map of Europe, she realized she could not locate the towns or villages where her ancestors came from, especially her great grandparents from her father's side, whose papers she has in her possession. She could not find all the places where they were born, married or died, as names of many cities and states have changed over the years. She started to ponder her family background and her Jewish heritage. This led to thoughts of Jewish history, rife with condemnations, segregations and hatred. She recalled the history of Columbus when he set out on his voyage by order of the Spanish Queen Isabella and King Ferdinand in 1492. The Jews of Spain were persecuted and forced to leave the country under threats of torture and death. Their belongings were confiscated by the Queen, who used them to finance the voyages of her fleets. Margot believes the saying, "Those who do not remember the past are condemned to relive it," is poignantly true.

She has learned a lot about herself by connecting with people. She especially recognizes that our lives are intertwined with the experiences of others. Nothing is a singular action, but is the result of the past and will affect the future. She has had a long, eventful journey and has always tried to look at life in a positive way. Even as a prisoner, she did not let the tragedy of her situation overwhelm her. She has attempted to look subjectively at the facts, added experiences to her memory and then continued on. This has made her the person she is today.

Margot's family history is rich in the tradition of

oral storytelling, and that is how she has always shared her story with others. Now, at age 87, she probed deeper into her memory to document her story. This has been very challenging and was done slowly and carefully. She has been afraid of failure and not being able to finish. At last, though, she has left something of herself behind that will give hope and encouragement to others.

So how did Margot explain the story of Auschwitz? She described another world where she lived - a world where all the rules were different. The standards of a civilized society did not exist. She tells of a gray world where nothing made sense. Where she was not even looked upon as a human being, but of a lowly, debased creature not worthy of dignity or respect. This has been her challenge as a survivor. It was a challenge to put her story into words. Until now, her story had been contained in her mind in pictures and feelings, unable to be documented in words that would accurately portray what she had experienced. But she felt she must convey to the world one more picture of the Holocaust. We must not forget what humanity is capable of; what humans can become and what crimes they can commit.

Margot adds her written account to those autobiographies so painfully shared by other survivors. World War II will never be forgotten. Those who died must be honored. Those who survived are an important part of that collective experience. Margot's hope is that her testimony of that horror will, in some small way, help to prevent the past from repeating itself. So she told the true story which she personally lived. Margot adds her testament to the others, so their experiences will not be forgotten: "I hope that it will do some good in the world."

Margot De Wilde

Name at birth: Ruth Margot Lustig; born in Berlin,
Germany, July 18, 1921.

Marriages:
1. 1942 Lodewyk Meyer, died 1944
2. 1951-1959 (div) Rein Woltz
3. 1961 Rudy DeWilde, died April 11, 2005

Mother: Ernestine (Erna) Baumblatt; born in Mainz,
Germany; Nov. 9, 1896 died June 28, 1969 in Amsterdam.

Father: Harry Lustig Born in Copenick, Germany; Sept. 6,
1888; died Nov. 3, 1967.

Brother: Rolf Dieter Manfred   Nicknames: Bubi, later
Manfred, later Peter (during and after war); 3-1/2 yrs
younger; married Hermiene Vecht; died Jan. 19, 1998.

Grandparents on mother's side came from Germany.
Grandparents on father's side from Bohemia,
Czechoslavakia.

Uncle: Ludwig (Erna's brother); wife Grete; their daughter
Inge.

Aunt: Bertha; mother took apparel course because of her.

Parents-in-law: Alex Meyer married to Flora Meyer. Sons

Philip, Lodewyk and John

Two friends in camp: Ann Vrachtdoender and Laura
Scheinderman

Chapter 1
Margot's Childhood

Ruth Margot Lustig had no idea that her comfortable world was about to change forever. On January 14, 1925, she was at her grandparents' apartment in Berlin, which was just one floor above the apartment she shared with her parents. She was merrily playing on their living room floor with her big, brown bear. It had wheels and, as she pushed it around, she was lost in the fantasies of her pretend world. She vaguely noticed the sweet smell coming from the bowl of fresh fruit on the table. She felt slight pangs of hunger, but did not worry about trivialities like that at three and a half years of age. Margot sensed something important was going on, but it was not a concern to dwell upon.

Margot and the rest of her Jewish family were living in Berlin, Germany. World War II was still a few years away. The war would bring about even bigger changes in her life, but right now a different sort of change was about to take place. During the past few weeks, everyone had been so busy! Margot's nanny, her parents and grandparents all seemed to be preoccupied. Not that she cared much, though. There were more important things to concern herself, like what to play with after she grew tired of her bear.

It was deceptively cold outside on that wintry day, as rays of sunlight shone through the windows onto the furniture. Margot was stuck indoors. Her grandparents did not often go outdoors in the middle of the winter. On this day, her parents had been gone since early morning. Just then, her grandfather happened to walk past her.

"Opa, kieks, kieks!" Margot squealed, knowing he couldn't resist her.

She flopped down on the floor to let Opa kneel down and tickle her belly, while he exclaimed in his kind voice, "Kieks kieks!"

Margot's grandparents and parents all had ways of showing endearments to her. They often did things that made her feel special. She felt much loved as a young child and did not realize that soon she would have to share their love.

That night, when Margot was sleeping in her room, she was suddenly awakened by her father, Harry. He was sitting on the bed next to her and a dim light from the hallway cast its glow into the room lighting his face. "Paps!" Margot cried, happy to see him again, as she had missed him that day. When he saw that she was awake, he kissed her and said, "Margot, your mother has just had a little baby brother for you." She was not too surprised by this news. She had heard her parents talking about it. It might be fun having a little brother, she thought as she drifted back to sleep.

The next day, Margot's father took her to a big building, which she later realized was a hospital, to see her mother and newborn brother. When they arrived, her mother, Erna, was lying on a bed with white sheets. She was holding a tiny figure wrapped in a blanket. "Margotlein, come greet your baby brother," Margot's mother instructed, calling her by her special nickname.

Margot skipped over and peered at the new little

being and breathed in his baby scent. She was amazed at how small he was, like one of her dolls. He was sleeping soundly and seemed so peaceful. "You must be very careful with him," her mother said. Margot did not realize it at the time, but thus began a sibling rivalry with her brother that would continue until they were teenagers. Fortunately, though, in later years she and her brother would grow very fond of each other.

Margot always believed her little brother, Manfred, was her mother's favorite. When they came home from the hospital, everyone was constantly talking about the cute "Bubi" ("little boy" in German), as he was nicknamed. Margot felt left out and awkward. From then on, he was always with Margot's mother. He could do no wrong, it seemed. Margot often thought that she unjustly received the blame for various infractions, with the remark, "You are older; you should know better." This brought much difficulty into her life as a child which, before then, had been idyllic. She could not have known then that there were much larger challenges looming in her future.

Margot has many memories of her childhood after her brother was born, and despite her jealousy of him, they are good memories. There was a park near their apartment, where Margot and her brother spent quite a lot of time with their Russian nanny, Olga. Margot's parents took them to the mountains of Austria and Bavaria during the summers and went on walks there. The family made day trips to Wannsee Lake, close to Berlin.

During the winters, they often went sledding. On one such sledding trip at a hilly forest in a suburb of Berlin when Margot was eight years old, she was sitting on the back of a bobsled, with some neighbor boys steering. Her parents were at the bottom of the hill with her little brother, and they were very worried that she might get injured. As Margot and the boys were coming down the hill, she was thrown off the sled and hit her head. She rode home on the subway in the arms of her father. Afterward, she spent many days recovering in a dark bedroom.

Margot does not remember being especially wild or clumsy as a child, but does recall the many times she had scrapes on her knees and legs. There was a back stairwell at her apartment in Berlin. It was used by the landlord, the servants and delivery people. The stairs went around and around from one floor to the other. The black steps were made of steel, with a rough surface to prevent them from being slippery. They were very noisy when walked upon. Playing there, without permission from her mother, Margot tumbled down many times, frequently hurting herself.

Toys were much simpler, but considered more beautiful and artfully constructed, than nowadays. Margot had a lovely dollhouse, with two rooms and a kitchen. It was complete with furniture, curtains and dinnerware. She had a small collection of dolls. She regrettably threw one favorite doll down the back stairway and broke it because she was angry at the time. Margot and Manfred had wooden interlocking building blocks, which they used to build castles and houses. When they were a little older, they played games with other kids, or had make-believe adventures like treasure hunts, improvised tennis courts on the street, and baseball games with scrap wood. And, like most children all over the world, they spent hours playing hide-and-seek. They made radios from pieces of string and empty yarn containers, and sent messages in code.

Music has always been an important part of

Margot's life. She has childhood memories of her parent's home, where opera, classical music and children's songs came from a strange box with a big horn on top. Of course, she later learned it was a record player. There are songs Margot would come to associate with an occurrence, like the "calling whistle" of her first love. She found out that the tune was the first line of the "Internationale," the national Communist anthem. In later years, certain parts of concerts, particularly the final movement from the Ninth Symphony of Beethoven, "Ode to Joy," and the "Moonlight Sonata," brought back memories of good times spent with her family.

Margot's grandfather on her mother's side was the owner of a department store in Mainz, and later Berlin, Germany. Margot's father worked there. Seven of her grandfather's fourteen children were still alive then; five girls and two boys. The boys became partners in the store. The dowry for the girls' at that time was the opportunity for their husbands to work in the department store. Margot's grandfather died when she was very young, and her mother's brother, Ludwig, his wife, Grete, and their daughter, Inge, moved in with her grandmother.

At this time in Germany, the economy was growing steadily worse. Leading to this point was Germany's defeat in World War I, which became official on Armistice Day, November 11, 1918. The Versailles Peace Treaty, which was signed on June 28, 1919, required Germans to make reparation payments to the Allies for damages. A commission was established that determined Germany's debt be set at 132 billion gold marks (approximately $31 billion at the current exchange rate). It was to be paid over a span of thirty-seven years at six percent interest. This, along with the debts which were incurred during the war, created an enormous financial burden on Germany that Adolf Hitler would later manipulate to his advantage. (2, 20)

In 1923, a hyperinflationary spiral hit Germany which financially ruined millions of Germans. With this crash of the German economy, the department store owned by Margot's family closed in the mid 1920's. Margot later learned that this meant that the dowries disappeared. Her father and uncles were on their own. Harry tried his hand at several other jobs, but did not have much success. Shortly after Margot's brother was born, her parent's financial state had degraded to the point where they could no longer afford to take many pictures of their children. Before Margot's brother was born, there were quite a few pictures taken of her, her nanny, grandparents and the apartment where they lived. But there are few existing pictures from the latter part of Margot's childhood.

As Margot and her brother grew older and went to school, the family's financial situation became very unpleasant because of the dire state of the economy. This caused the family to make changes in their lifestyle, such as letting the nanny go. After several failures at various jobs, Margot's father found work with a friend of the family as a sales representative. The family moved to Hamburg for a year, but when the firm went bankrupt in 1928 they returned to Berlin.

Because of a recommendation from his brother, Gustav, who was already in Holland working as a buyer for a department store, Harry was offered a job with a German firm stationed in Amsterdam. He accepted the job, moved there and lived with his brother and family. He worked as a representative of German factories and travelled often to Denmark, Sweden, and Norway. When he returned home to visit his family in Berlin on weekends, it always caused much excitement. He brought money and gifts for his family, but, better than that, he entertained them with his storytelling.

One of the methods that the Nazi party employed at this time to gain support for their political party was to recruit young Germans, as they were considered to be impressionable and spirited. The Hitler Jugend (HJ; Hitler Youth) was established in 1926 and continued to grow steadily. In 1939, membership in this and its companion organization, the Bund Deutscher Madel (BDM; League of German Girls), became compulsory and membership reached almost nine million Germans between ten and eighteen years of age. At the end of 1931, while she was still in Berlin, Margot's mother had an encounter with a group of young people who were involved in the Nazi youth movement. They were heckling people and demonstrating. This was a very frightening experience for Erna. She decided that she no longer felt safe in Germany. She said to her husband, "Listen, I don't feel safe here with two kids. You see to it that we get to Holland, too."

Harry arranged to have Margot, her mother and brother move to Holland in 1932, when Margot was almost eleven years old. For Margot, this was a heartbreaking departure from all things familiar. She loved Berlin, where she had spent the first youthful years of her life and had many friends whom she loved. She did not want to leave and resisted the move. When Erna took Margot and Manfred to the train station to leave Germany, Margot did not make it easy for her.

"Come on, kids, stop fussing," her mother said wearily.

"Why?" Margot asked.

"We are going to see Daddy - to be with him."

"Why?" she asked again, to be more disagreeable.

"You know he has not been here for a while."

"Yes."

"We are going to live in Holland."

"Where is that?"

"Far away, where Uncle Gustav lives."

"I don't want to."

"Don't you want to be with Daddy?"

"Yes, but I want to be with my friends."

"You will make new friends there."

"I don't want to."

"Stop this; come on. We've got to go."

"I hate you; I don't want to go away!"

"Daddy will be there, waiting for us."

"I'm tired," Margot whined.

"That's enough now. Come on. Will someone help me get these kids onto the train?" Erna asked with exasperation - to no one in particular.

So in June, 1932, Margot and her family moved to Amsterdam and lived for a while with Uncle Gustav and his family. Margot and Manfred attended school there and quickly learned the Dutch language. Margot was fortunate because her mother had found a special school for her which she enjoyed. The school was structured with a "task" system, similar to a Montessori school. The students were given weekly tasks in various subjects, which they could finish at their own pace. When they were all completed, they could do what they wanted with the remaining time. The teacher provided help as needed. Margot made new friends. Much of their playtime was spent outdoors on an empty lot. They also played in the streets and open fields. Improvised hockey, tennis, and hide and seek were favorite games.

It was a stressful, yet an easy, life because Margot was still too young to see troubles. There was not a lot of anti-Semitism in Holland at that time. Yet it was difficult for them as immigrants. They were not fully accepted by the Dutch, even Jews. The Dutch greatly resented the German immigrants, as they felt that jobs were being taken away from them. But there were other immigrant children there, too. They befriended many other German Jewish kids.

By 1932, the National Socialist Party (Nazis) had become the largest political party in Germany. Anti-Semitism had been simmering in Germany for centuries. Now, because of economic reasons, it had reached a boiling point. Germans wanted decisive leadership and national rebirth. President Paul von Hindenburg, aged 85, saw no better solution and fearing continued chaos, reluctantly appointed Hitler as chancellor of Germany on January 30, 1933. That way, Hitler could be controlled and order could be restored. But this was not to be. Half a year after becoming chancellor, democracy in Germany was dead and Hitler had gained power. Hitler blamed the Jews for Germany's defeat in World War I and the current state of the German economy. He continued to grow in popularity among the German people and spread anti-Semitic views. He became absolute dictator of Germany in August, 1934, when President von Hindenburg died. (2, 53-54)

Margot's father, Harry, lost his income in 1934,

when the economy continued to grow worse and the Dutch and other countries began boycotting German products. Margot's family moved almost every year, because they no longer had any decent income and thus were qualified to receive free rent for the first few months after each move. Frequent moves were common for low-income families.

When Margot was thirteen, in 1934, she began helping with the homemaking and took odd jobs like sewing and babysitting in order to help her parents financially. She began bicycling on a bike which she rented for the equivalent of ten cents an hour. She had quite a few tumbles before catching on to cycling. Finally, she saved enough money to purchase a secondhand bike which had tires that developed leaks at almost every street corner. She became quite adept at repairing these on the spot. She used two old kitchen spoons and glue, assisted by the ever-present hand pump which was clipped onto the bike. Margot's bicycle became her mode of transportation, using it almost daily to travel to friends' houses and the store, as it had a basket in front.

In 1935, Margot's mother received an invitation from her sister, who was still living in Berlin, to travel there to take a course in making intimate apparel for heavyset persons. These products were not available on the market at the time. Erna's sister was married to a Swiss person; therefore, she was not subjugated to the prohibitions imposed on Jews. Erna accepted the invitation from her sister. She took the course and was then able to build a nice business in Holland. Margot's father did the administrative bookkeeping and housework.

Harry did most of the cooking for the family and, by helping him, Margot learned how to cook. Desserts were made from scratch: cream of wheat with raisins, rice puddings, or dried fruits. In addition, fruit salads were made from blemished fruits from the green grocer. Margot and her father had a special fondness for soups, which were also made from scratch. They gave special attention to the preparation. It was mostly her nose which guided Margot into culinary creativity. She still has a strong association with certain scents reminding her of home, her parents and even her grandparents.

Margot finished elementary school and then attended an art school. By age fifteen, she had to quit school to devote more time to care for the household. She often had to tell the grocery delivery boy, "My mother will pay you tomorrow. She's not here." They simply did not have the money to pay him. Those were very hard times, yet Erna continued to build her business clientele so she was able to support the family.

Margot's family kept some of the Jewish holidays, but religion was never a significant part of her life as a child. Her parents were members of a Reformed synagogue, and they did not keep a kosher kitchen. Margot was in a Girl Scout group and then later in a Jewish youth group at the Reformed synagogue where she became the secretary. When the Queen Mother of Holland died, Margot wrote a letter to the Royal House sending their condolences. She received a letter in return, thanking them.

She landed a job categorizing and organizing the library of a publisher. The pay was 1/10th of a guilder an hour (equivalent to a dime an hour). She was allowed to keep her earnings, but had to buy things for herself, such as clothing. She eventually collected enough money to purchase new tires for her precarious bicycle. She felt very proud, going into a bike shop in Amsterdam, to make the purchase of two tires at almost a guilder apiece. She can still remember the smell of the store; a smell of rubber.

Margot says, "It was a hard time, but yet it was a good time, because we learned to appreciate things." Best of all, she and her family were still together.

Musings with Margot. . .

SLW: How did your life change after your brother was born?

RMD: After my brother was born, I turned into a very grouchy little girl. I was envious. My brother was cute looking, younger, and I always heard, 'You should know better, you are the older one.' So he was blamed for nothing and I always received the blame. And there was so much talk about his good looks, and I felt like I had my mouth from ear to ear.

SLW: Do you remember much about the Catholic school you attended?

RMD: I remember vaguely the Catholic school in Berlin. There were statues of saints up and down the hallways and it smelled like incense. And in the morning we prayed in class. I prayed in the Jewish way with folded hands, like I was instructed to do, and the other children prayed as they were told, by making the sign of the cross. It was not that I was in a Catholic school by choice. I happened to live in the district of Berlin which was mainly Catholic."

CLM: Describe the art school that you attended.

RMD: It was a regular school that also had specialized art classes. I liked drawing, even architectural drawing. I liked clothes designing and metal design; scrollwork for doors and other metals.

CLM: Did you attend a synagogue with your parents when you were a child?

RMD: On High Holy days I went with them. Rosh Hashanah and Yom Kippur. We joined in group festivities like any church has on special days. But nothing especially religious. Mostly people who considered themselves German Jews were in this Reformed synagogue. Because, as is typical of German Judaism, they were German first and the religion of Judaism was secondary. Other people say they are Jewish Americans. But my family and the people we knew were Germans with a connection to a synagogue. And in the synagogue, the services were partly in Hebrew and then parts of the prayers were in German or Dutch.

Letters to Margot

"When I see the letters of others, it is so incredible - the impact of my speeches which people write to me about. And then I think, 'Well, somewhere along the line I might have done something right.' I'm very touched every time someone writes, 'I will tell my children'."

Margot

Dear Mrs. DeWilde,
Thank you so very much for coming to speak with us and giving us a first-hand account of your experiences. You are a very nice, genuine and funny woman. It was very eye-opening to hear about your life. I thought it was cool when you told us about how you played sports and games. Thank you so much again!

Elise

Chapter 2
The Pre-War Buildup

In the early years of the Nazi regime, national laws were instituted that would define, segregate and impoverish the German Jews. They were gradually separated from non-Jewish society and their freedom was increasingly restricted. There were limits placed on the percentage of Jewish students allowed in German schools and universities. Jews were banned from German sports organizations and they were driven from their government jobs and professions. These restrictions were enacted to force Jewish citizens to flee Germany, while leaving most of their possessions behind. Many Jews left Germany to seek better lives in other countries. This became difficult, though, as restrictions on travel increased and other countries limited immigration. Also, many other Jewish citizens decided to stay put, rather than seek asylum elsewhere, because of their loyalty to Germany. They were confident Hitler and his Nazi Party would soon be voted out of office and the hard times would pass. No one could have imagined what was yet to come.

Up until 1938, Jewish people in Germany were occasionally still granted permission to go on vacations with their own money. Margot's Aunt Elsa, who was her father's sister, sometimes travelled with her son to Amsterdam, Holland, and took Margot or her brother with her to her hotel. During one of those times, Margot was staying with her aunt at a Jewish hotel and was reading on the terrace. Two young men happened to stroll by, one of whom Margot knew from a Jewish youth group. He came over and introduced his companion, Lodewyk. They asked if she would like to go for a walk with them and she agreed. She was uncomfortable at the time, as she was wearing her first store-bought bra. She was very self-conscious about this, so she walked with her arms crossed in front of her. Margot and Lodewyk, nicknamed Lo, became friends. They found that they shared the same philosophies. They both believed in Zionism and wanted to go to Israel someday and raise children.

Lo was two years her senior and was going to a university to get his master's degree when Margot met him. His plan was to become an agricultural advisor in Israel (which was Palestine at the time). He was a Misrahiest (Zionist) and was a devout Jew from a Reformed family. When things started to change in Germany, he changed his views about religion. He became strictly Orthodox (keeping a kosher kitchen, restricting all activities on the Sabbath, eating only at kosher restaurants, etc.).

Lo lived at the university near Arnhem and came to see Margot on the weekends when he came to visit his parents. It was awhile before she met them, though. When she and Lo first met, he still had a girlfriend in Switzerland. Margot did not learn about this right away, and Lo had to bring that relationship to an end before anything with Margot could be steady. In order to keep Margot a secret from his parents until he was ready to tell them about her, Margot would not tell his parents who she was when she called him on the phone. She just asked, "Is Lo home?" Lo simply told them that she was his friend.

Lo eventually told his parents about Margot, and his

Father urged him to introduce her to them when they were on the town one evening. His father said to him, "Now you go and walk on the boulevard and Mom and I will come from the opposite direction. When we all meet, you can finally introduce your girl to us."

Lo's parents were very prominent people in the community. As Margot got to know Lo's father, Alex Meyer, she found he was a generous man with a big heart. He became a mentor to her during the brief time she knew him. She tried to live her life the way he did. He inspired her by being what she considered to be a mensch, "a person of integrity and rectitude." She regarded him as a humanitarian who was extremely wise.

Mr. Meyer was a self-made man who had become the largest textile distributor in the Netherlands. He was very wealthy; the family had a car, a chauffeur and a summer house. He helped many victims during the depression. Margot saw him buy goods from people; odds and ends, none of which he ever had any use for. But in making purchases, he gave people the feeling of having done something for the money they received, rather than accepting charity.

In Germany, Hitler continued to threaten and impose more restrictions. Jewish citizens had to wear the yellow star at all times on their outerwear. They were allowed to only shop at certain stores, at designated times; they could not gather in public anymore; they were banned from using public transportation. All Jewish students were expelled from German schools and were only allowed to attend Jewish schools. Participation in the economy was severely restricted. The people allowed to leave the country had to leave their possessions behind. By then, all Jews had been forced to register assets exceeding 5000 marks and any real estate they owned. This made it very risky to say they did not have anything of value and then take it with them. German Jews were ordered to surrender all silver and gold to government authorities. The confiscation of Jewish valuables and properties became the primary source of funding for the German military, as laid out in Hitler's book Mein Kampf.

In Holland, there were no restrictions; everybody was still free to do as they wanted. Therefore, citizens were not generally affected by the changes taking place in Germany. Dutch citizens hoped that the storm of discrimination in Germany soon would pass.

On September 1, 1939, World War II began when Germany invaded western Poland. Warsaw was bombed, killing three thousand Jewish civilians. On September 3, 1939, Great Britain and France declared war on Germany. This prevented Polish Jews from immigrating to England because all visas were cancelled. German forces continued to take over and occupy Polish territories. Within three weeks, Poland was conquered by the German army.

Jews were restricted to ghettos created in Germany and Poland. Many, from small towns and villages, were taken to larger cities and imprisoned in an area of the city that was sectioned off. Conditions in these ghettos were brutal. The people who were forced to live there had to deal with starvation and overcrowding. The practice of Jewish religion was outlawed, so they worshipped in secret. A Judenrat (Jewish council) was established in each of the ghettos. The assigned leaders were forced to obey the demands of the Nazis. They were made personally responsible for enforcing all Nazi orders. They supervised the movements from their homes to the ghettos.

In September, 1939, Holland mobilized. Holland is below sea level, with many of the houses built on stilts. Part of Holland's defense system was to open the levies so the country would be partly underwater. They also planned to demolish critical bridges across key rivers leading into Holland, in order to slow the German advance. The Germans planned to capture the bridges across Holland's rivers and canals, and then invade the Netherlands before the Dutch could flood the land.

After the defeat of Poland, the Germans invaded Holland on May 10, 1940. They struck with thousands of bi-planes which dropped parachutists, many of whom were dressed in civilian clothing. They camouflaged themselves as professionals, nursemaids with buggies, and many other types of civilians. Some were even dressed in Dutch military uniforms which they had stolen the previous year from a train they had intercepted. Dutch radio stations sent broadcasts all day long announcing to the people where parachutists had landed. To confuse the Germans, the Dutch removed many of the road signs.

Within the first few hours of the German campaign, most major installations were assaulted by the Luftwaffe (the German Air Force). That year, Margot was living in a kibbutz north of Amsterdam near the connecting channel between Amsterdam and the North Sea port. The Germans began bombing Rotterdam and threatened that if Holland did not surrender, the same fate would befall the entire country. Queen Wilhelmina and her parliament fled to England by ship.

The fast-moving Panzer tanks combined with heavy bombardment by the Luftwaffe were too much for the defenders. Even though critical bridges were destroyed and areas flooded, the Germans overcame these obstacles much quicker than the Dutch had anticipated. It took only four days of war before Holland capitulated. Even after the surrender, though, Dutch troops continued to fight for a few more days in scattered locations throughout Holland with artillery support from the Royal Navy. The Dutch inflicted heavy casualties on the Germans during this brief but fierce campaign.

The Dutch initially expected the Allied armies would drive the Germans back and they would soon be liberated. This was not to be, however. Allied forces in France were forced into Britain. The ones remaining surrendered when Germany became victor at the Battle of France. The Dutch then resigned themselves to the eventuality that the Nazi occupation was not temporary.

Shortly after the victory, the Germans proposed that the Dutch government return from exile and collaborate with the Nazis. Queen Wilhelmina refused, though, and Holland was placed under the control of a German civilian governor. This civil government was headed by Nazi politician Arthur Seyss-Inquart, who had already been successful in turning Jews in Austria into second-class citizens. He, along with other German officials including Adolf Hitler, considered the Dutch to be part of the Aryan Herrenvolk (elite). One of their goals was to assimilate the non-Jewish Dutch citizens into the greater Germanic nation they were trying to build.

At the beginning of the German occupation in Holland, the citizens did not notice much change. But gradually, more and more actions were implemented against Jews to eliminate them from society. A policy of

Gleichschaltung ("enforced conformity") was implemented, which systematically eliminated non-Nazi organizations.

After a short time, the Germans ordered a prominent group of Jewish people to form a Jewish counsel, just as they did in Germany. They were instructed to fulfill all the orders the Germans did not want to carry out themselves. Newspapers publicized the orders, one of which was to have everyone in Holland registered. Registration had been instigated by Napoleon in the 1800s, so the system of voluntary registration had already been established. Everyone was given a new registration card, which looked like a double-sided driver's license. It had a picture on one side with the city stamp near the picture, and on the other side a fingerprint along with name, address and sometimes a profession. The Jewish people had a large "J" printed on the front of theirs. Thus, the Germans had a method of identifying Jewish people whenever they wanted to segregate them.

The Jews in Holland were now being subjected to the same restrictions that had been implemented in Germany. They were no longer allowed to have radios. They were ordered to surrender their bicycles and jewelry. Bank accounts were controlled. They could no longer go to the movies, use a streetcar, go swimming or use a sports facility. There were no remaining public places left where they could go except during times designated for Jews only. The Nazis tried to move Jews into ghettos by forcing them into areas of the city. However, most Jews continued to live in their own homes until they were ordered to report for relocation or taken in raids.

During the raids, Nazis would block off a street at both ends and inspect identification cards. Certain people were selected who were then herded onto trucks and taken away. Their valuables were confiscated. Young people were often sent to labor camps. These camps were created by the Germans for large projects which required a steady supply of manual labor.

Jews in Holland were given big, yellow stars with "Jood" (Jew) printed on them. They were ordered to sew the stars onto their outerwear. The stars were required to be visible whenever they ventured out. Their shopping was restricted to certain times of day. When it was not a designated Jewish shopping time, they could not go into a store with their star showing. Of course, many people resisted this degrading regulation by hiding their stars and continuing to shop when they pleased. Margot did this often, despite the possible consequences of being caught. Rather than being nervous, she felt anger towards the new regime that was infringing on her liberties.

Margot's father heard that someone from their neighborhood threatened to call the police if Margot was ever seen again without a star. The police would then inform the Nazis. Therefore, she was forced to wear the star in her neighborhood. As soon as she left the area, though, she took off her coat, put it over her arm and went about her normal business. She never learned the name of the informant. She had a slight suspicion that it was the man who had once rented a room in their house. Although he was Jewish, he was rumored to be working for the Gestapo.

Twice, Margot found herself caught in the middle of raids. Each time, instead of being overcome by fear, she boldly approached a German officer and asked for directions to specific streets. Each time, she was escorted toward the locations. She never had any trouble doing this, because her looks did not give her away. Since she spoke fluent German, they did not suspect she was Jewish. However, her father, who had false papers, was checked several times. Fortunately, though, his falsification was never detected.

Lo's family and Margot decided they would leave Holland. They applied for papers that would allow them to immigrate to the United States. They received their papers the day before Japan bombed Pearl Harbor, Hawaii, in December, 1941. Then, America declared war on Japan and Germany. All immigration to the United States was stopped at that point. They were unable to escape to America.

Margot's Reflections. . .

SLW: Were the non-Jewish people in Holland sympathetic, for the most part, to the Jews?

RMD: For the most part, yes, because there was not much anti-Semitism. But at that time, there was a lot of unemployment in Holland. So there was a little bit of begrudging that other people came in to make their chances of finding work even less.

SLW: Were you aware of what was going on in Germany; how the Jews were being treated?

RMD: We learned of what was happening there. We heard about the kristallnacht when they smashed all the store windows of the Jewish people, and of the book burning. By having relatives there, you learned what was going on by correspondence. Later, we had some relatives come to Holland after we were there; a sister of my mother and her family. They did everything like it was the most normal thing to do. And in Germany when they started accusing people of mixed marriage, Jewish and non-Jewish Germans, the youngest brother of my mother committed suicide because he didn't want his non-Jewish wife to suffer for him. In Germany, they got wise of everything happening so much earlier than we did in Holland. We lived our lives, with misery around us.

CLM: What was your experience of living in a kibbutz

like? What made you decide to live there?

RMD: I had to learn Orthodox housekeeping because I was from a Reformed family. I didn't know any of these things, and I had to learn some Orthodox ways in order to do the right thing for my husband later. That's what I went to the kibbutz for. But Lo was a person who had voluntarily chosen to be religious, Orthodox. They did old-fashioned things like separating meat and milk; sanitary and maybe at that time logical things. And of course if you start changing, then eventually the original religion disappears and it becomes something else. And I think that's why some people really hang on to the old way, in order to have it not die out.

CLM: When did you live in the kibbutz?

RMD: In 1939, for a little more than half a year.

CLM: Were you able to see Lo while you were there?

RMD: Not very often. In this group of youngsters, I fell in love with one of the guys. I decided Lo was not paying enough sentimental attention to me. So I decided to call it off. I am a person who needs little signs of attention. He never sent anything or brought anything to me while I was living in the kibbutz. He never thought of little gifts, and that was the big stumbling block for me, that he never showed any sentimental attention. Lo went to my father and my father convinced him that it wasn't so serious, and gave him some advice. Then I got a big package with all kinds of things; a pair of gloves, a ring and a letter. So we made up.

I thought I was in love with that other guy, but it was not serious. I felt attracted to him. Lo stayed with me, though, which is something to be thankful for.

CLM: Did you enjoy your time at the kibbutz?
RMD: It was a lot of working. Three girls took care of thirty people. And we had a wood-fired stove. We did not have hot water. If you needed hot water you had to heat it. I worked at a farm for a little while in the spring picking strawberries and learning to milk cows. And the money I made went to the communal kitty. We spoke Hebrew on Saturdays. I don't remember much of it anymore. My life must have been very superficial. I didn't take things too seriously at the time and didn't think things through.

Dear Mrs. DeWilde,
Thank you very much for sharing your story. I enjoyed hearing about you and your husband and the tough decisions you faced. Hearing you speak really helped me to understand the Holocaust better.

Dan

Ms. DeWilde,
I love your accent. Also, it's amazing you do not have a drop of hate in your heart...

Mike

Chapter 3
Dutch Love and Marriage

Alex Meyer, Lo's father, was in poor health and was told by his doctor he had to cut down on many of his favorite indulgences. He was an epicurean who enjoyed rich food, a good cigar, and a glass of cognac. His doctor told him he could no longer partake of these luxuries. Friday nights were especially festive, which included a large family meal. After the bad news from the doctor, he resigned himself to a bowl of vegetables or salad for dinner. He endured it only a few days, and then finally said, "To hell with it! Then I die earlier! I'm not going to live like that anymore!" So from then on, he had his cognac and cigar and whatever foods he desired. Alex Meyer passed away in November, 1941, from angina pectoris at the age of fifty-three. He died as Margot held him in her arms, surrounded by his wife, mother-in-law and three sons. He was spared the grief that would later befall his family.

After Mr. Meyer died, Margot and Lo became engaged to be married. Margot moved away from her family's apartment to live with Lo, his mother and two older brothers. She shared a bedroom with Lo's mother, Flora. At that time people generally had two ceremonies – the official, state marriage and the religious ceremony. In April, 1942, Lo and Margot were officially married by the burgermeister (mayor) of Wageningen. This was a town with its own rules, where Lo was attending an agricultural university. In Amsterdam they would have had to go to an

administrative building where only Jews were "handled."
By holding the ceremony where they did, they were able to
have a pleasant, normal wedding. Even with restrictions on
travel, her parents attended the wedding.

Upon returning to Amsterdam on their wedding
night, Margot and Lo were talking in the living room
when they heard Lo's mother call out, "Margot, aren't
you coming to bed?" Flora expected that Margot would
continue to share a bedroom with her. This was agreeable
to Margot and Lo, though, because they did not consider
this to be their real wedding day. At this time, Lo was
twenty-three and Margot was twenty-one. Their plan was
that when Lo had his Doctorate and the war was over,
they would have their official religious wedding. They
were married just for the sake of having the same name,
in the hopes of being able to stay together if something
unforeseen should happen. Also, Margot would be
protected for the time being from deportation because Lo
was teaching Jewish youth groups.

Lo and Margot often discussed their plans for the
future. She wanted to accompany him to Israel, where they
hoped to raise six children. After getting married, Margot
had to obtain an identification card with her new last name
on it. When she arrived at the town hall, the official handed
her a new card without a "J." She had heard of a threat to
mixed marriages. She thought that she could not take such
a risk. She brought attention to the fact that the official did
not put a "J" on the card. She later realized that she could
have kept the card without the "J," then come back later
to inform them she had lost her card and be issued a new
one with a "J." This would have given her the option of
passing as a non-Jew. But at the time, she was afraid that

her actions would endanger her husband.

Many people were told by letter to report to a certain building, at a certain time and were instructed to bring only one suitcase. Margot's brother Manfred received a letter to present himself at a labor camp in September, 1942. The Lustig family took this as a sign to go underground. Manfred went first, then their parents. Most families who went into hiding during the war stayed together. Margot and her family, though, decided that it would be safer for them to separate. They also deliberately avoided any knowledge of each other's locations. They planned it this way in case they were ever questioned about the locations of the others.

Manfred's first hiding place turned out to be unsafe, so he returned to the Meyer's family. Later, he and Margot's mother went into hiding on a farm in the country. After that, they were both evacuated and went to the room in Arnhem that Margot and Lo had previously rented and furnished. This is where they remained until liberation. Margot's Father found a place with colleagues in Amsterdam with whom he used to play cards. Although his family did not know the location of his hiding place, there was an in-between person, a Danish woman, through whom Margot could contact him.

Since Margot's family was going into hiding, this meant, as in Germany, most of their possessions had to be left behind. Her father had obtained false papers and spoke German, so he dared to go several times to their house and remove valuables. He gathered papers and pictures which he took to his hiding place. Many of these Margot still has today.

Most of the belongings that all Jews had to leave

behind were taken away by a "moving company" called Puls. This company was hired by the German government to collect furniture and goods from all the homes of Jews who were transported. The Jewish property was confiscated and the money used to support the Third Reich programs, pay government debts and fund the war. Margot and her mother had hidden some valuables under the floor of their bathroom. But a renter of theirs, a protected Jew who worked for the Nazis (the same one, Margot suspects, who earlier had threatened to inform on her), found what they had concealed. Margot was later told by some neighbors that he had taken those goods to sell in their neighborhood.

Margot was frustrated about what was happening, but realized she could do nothing about it. As a nonconformist, she wanted to do whatever she was told not to do. She tried to resist all that was imposed on her. She always acted in the spirit of opposition. Many Jewish people had numbed themselves to the threat of the Third Reich. They hoped that they could escape to a different country and begin a new life. Some Jews were able to immigrate to Palestine and other countries.

Margot has very few detailed memories of that time. She does remember that, while resisting the present, she tried to think about a happy future. No one at that time imagined what would happen. The future was very uncertain.

Tea and Talk. . .

SLW: What are some of the favorite things that you and Lo used to do together?

RMD: We mostly talked. Once we went to a Hasidic get together, with dancing. We worked in the garden at his parent's house. Sometimes we went to a concert or a movie. We spent most of the time making plans, having illusions about things, the way that the world should be, and what we would do.

SLW: Did you become very close to Lo's brothers?

RMD: We didn't have much to do with them. They had their girls, their lives. They were older so they didn't want to have anything to do with the younger brother. So we didn't have much contact with them.

CLM: You said you had heard of the threat to mixed marriages – what was the threat?

RMD: Well, they arrested the Jewish part of the mixed marriage. It was an instinctive thought when I was given the card without the "J." My first thought was, "No, I can't do that. It would put Lo in danger." But it wouldn't have, because nobody would have known that I had the card. So there are instinctive things which you do in life, which at the time you think are right but sometimes would have been wiser had you acted differently.

Dear Margot DeWilde,

. . . You are an amazing woman. I really look up to you for all of your strength. One thing that I found to be so interesting was that if you would have left the "J" off the paper you would have probably not have had to go to Auschwitz. Instead, you thought of your husband. That is so admirable and respectful of you. You are truly an amazing woman!

Molly

Chapter 4
Resistance

Throughout the entire Holocaust many people, both Jewish and non-Jewish, resisted the Third Reich, and defied and fought back against their oppressors in many ways. Much of the evidence for this comes from documents and testimonies of survivors. Resistance took place as the restrictions on Jews increased in the ghettos, forests and death camps. This resistance took many forms. Some people broke the new laws whenever they felt they could get away with it. Some went into hiding; others escaped. Some groups even revolted in the ghettos and concentration camps. Many Nazis were killed. Mostly, though, resistance took the form of small, independent groups that produced counterfeit money and forged ration and identification cards. They also produced genuine and false maps, printed underground newspapers and distributed food and goods to those in need.

Some Dutch citizens collaborated and helped the Germans after their takeover in Holland. These people profited greatly. But there were also many who consistently opposed the Germans and helped the Jews. The underground counter-intelligence and domestic sabotage provided support to Allied forces. Communication networks were also established that helped lead to the eventual liberation of Holland. Some resisted in seemingly more insignificant ways. They shared their food with Jews who were hiding in the woods or passing through.

The personal risk for any resistance was immense. Some people, such as those who helped Margot's family, took Jews into their homes to hide. This aid was punishable by death.

Soon after getting married, Margot became involved in a resistance group through a neighbor. They helped with the falsification of identification papers. Sometimes the members of this resistance group stole identification cards from people in a crowd, but mostly the cards were obtained from volunteer donors. Some citizens freely gave their cards, and then later claimed them as being lost. They were issued new cards.

The pictures on the cards obtained by the resistance group were then soaked off. Margot helped by replacing the pictures and falsifying the city marks to make them look real. Lo was not involved. He did not have false identification papers, because he had recognizable Jewish features – he felt he could not pass as a non-Jew. Margot, on the other hand, was easily able to pass as a non-Jewish person and often carried her false papers. Later during the war, Margot found out that some members of the group were captured and executed.

The Joodse Raad (Jewish Counsel) that the Germans had established in the Netherlands first met in February, 1941. It swiftly became a powerful presence in Holland with responsibilities including the management of Jewish agencies and schools. It was also in charge of the distribution of food and types of certificates, such as travel permits. The counsel published the periodical Het Joodse Weekblad (The Jewish Weekly). It took over a finance committee that had been previously formed, which collected taxes that were imposed on Jews. In August,

1941, Jews were ordered to deposit their money in the Lippmann-Rosenthal bank, where contributions for the counsel were also deposited. The Joodse Raad was heavily criticized by many Jews for their cooperation with the Nazis. Their cooperation, though, was only given because of the threats to themselves and others if they did not obey.

In 1941, steps were implemented in Holland to lead to the "Final Solution," the Nazi's plan to totally annihilate European Jews and all other groups deemed undesirable by the Third Reich. The Joodse Raad was forced to carry out orders given by the Nazis. In the Netherlands, they had to organize and implement the movement of Dutch Jews into concentration camps and coordinate the movement of Jews to labor camps. The members of the counsel were given the horrific duty of selecting which unfortunate individuals would be deported to the camps. They were ordered to help facilitate the deportations.

So far in Europe, the Nazis' plan to destroy all Jews had begun by moving Jews to ghettos and allowing them to starve to death. Then, in 1941, as plans were leading to the invasion of Russia, four mobile killing units which were collectively called Einsatzgruppen ("Special Duty Groups") were formed in the east. Comprised of three thousand men, they rounded up Jews for "resettlement" and transported them to secluded execution spots. The Jews were ordered to relinquish their valuables, were forced to remove their clothing, and were killed. The victims were often forced to dig their own mass graves before being put to death. About 1.3 million Jews were executed by the Einsatzgruppen during that year. (2)

Hitler had already begun, in 1939, a euthanasia ("mercy killing") program which involved putting to death mentally or physically handicapped Germans, many of whom were children. These so-called "imperfect Aryans" were at first given deadly injections. Later, Hitler ordered experimentations with gas, and they began to be killed using that method. After about a year, the euthanasia program was stopped due to the outcry of the German people and church officials. But after this, Reinhard Heydrich and Adolf Eichmann, top Nazi officials, felt that the pace of destruction by the Einsatzgruppen was too slow. They ordered the building of the first death camps. Hitler had given them the duty of eliminating the Jews of Europe as efficiently and quietly as possible.

Pogroms already had been taking place in all occupied countries of Europe, not only by the Einsatzgruppen but by smaller Nazi killing squads as well, when the first concentration camps were established. Dachau was the first concentration camp. It was established by Heinrich Himmler, Hitler's deputy and head of the SS, in March, 1933. At first, it included Communists, Social Democrats, and other political enemies, who were to be "concentrated" there. The categories of camp inmates were expanded in the middle to late 1930s, and came to include "habitual criminals." These "antisocial elements" included Gypsies, beggars, vagrants, the mentally ill, homosexuals, Jehovah's Witnesses and, most of all, Jewish people.

In the Chelmno, Poland, death camp, victims perished from deadly gas that was piped into sealed mobile trucks. Auschwitz, Treblinka, Belzec and Sobibor began receiving large numbers of people who were put to death in gas chambers. A non-Jewish friend of Margot's father, who was married to a Jewish woman, passed along stories about gas chambers at death camps. But, for the most part, there were not many rumors being spread. Jews were told that non-Aryans were unwanted in parts of Europe so they would, therefore, be relocated. After her brother received his order for deportation (September, 1942), Margot knew it was time for the rest of her family to go into hiding. Since they did not know what atrocities had actually been taking place, they tried to remain optimistic.

By November, 1942, Margot's mother had been in hiding for about two months. Margot's parents still did not know the location of each other's hiding places. Margot knew that her mother was with a family who lived on a farm somewhere in the country. Margot knew the location of the Danish woman, through whom she could contact her father. This woman suggested that Margot and her father go visit Erna to celebrate her birthday. Margot met with her father and together they travelled without stars, carrying false papers. They took a train to Utrecht, about twenty minutes from Amsterdam, where they waited to board another train.

While they were at the station in Utrecht, her father told Margot not to look around because someone was staring at her. After a while, Margot dared to glance back. There stood a girl who had been in the kibbutz with her. She was dressed as a peasant, with drab clothes. They exchanged smiles and walked toward each other, but did not recall each other's names. They spent a few pleasant moments together, talking and joking. Then each went her own way. Margot and her father boarded a slowpoke train that took them to the city near the farm where her mother was hiding.

When they arrived at the farm they celebrated

Erna's birthday. Margot's mother had never learned to speak Dutch well; she had difficulty pronouncing words in Dutch. This made the prospect of her posing as a Dutch non-Jewish citizen very difficult. Margot overcame this by printing on her mother's false papers "Speech Impairment." The people she was staying with at the farm introduced her as a poor family member from Rotterdam, which had been bombed. When anyone questioned them, they explained that the shock of the bombing had caused her to lose her power of speech. This worked well, because otherwise she would have been immediately detected as not being Dutch. This was the last time Margot saw her mother until after the war. Her father went his own way after the celebration. Occasionally, he was able to visit Margot at her in-laws. He did not do this often, though, because of the great risk of being in public. The crime of posing as a non-Jew was punishable by death. He remained active and went shopping for necessities occasionally, without his star. But mostly he stayed in the apartment in Amsterdam where he was hiding.

Before the war, Margot and Lo rented a room in a boardinghouse near the university, while he was still allowed to attend. While he was studying agriculture there, he sometimes went on field trips with his professor. What Margot did not know was that her in-laws gave Lo a large sum of money for safeguarding. Lo continued to rent the room even though they left the boardinghouse. Later, an unidentified friend arranged for Margot's brother to live in the boardinghouse because he could no longer hide at the farm. Later, when the rural area where Erna was hiding was evacuated, she joined Manfred in hiding at the boardinghouse. So Erna and Manfred were reunited for a while and the money from Lo's family continued to pay their room and board.

As countless numbers of Jews continued to be deported from the country, the Joodse Raad continued unsuccessfully to negotiate the release of the Jews. In 1943, the council was forced to provide a list of 7,000 Jews from its employees and their families. The orders were sent to all the Jews on the list, but only about ten percent of them reported for deportation. This signified the end of the council's power over the Jewish community. Many people, by then, had gone into hiding or found other ways to avoid the orders for deportation. By the end of the year, all the remaining members of the Joodse Raad were included for deportation.

Many of Margot's friends and relatives were not fortunate enough to find a way out of the country or a hiding place. Many others trusted that it really was "relocation," as the Germans called it. They followed the orders for deportation. Disbelief was prevalent among the Dutch, Jews and non-Jews alike, about what was being done in concentration camps. Rumors circulated about where the people who were deported were taken. Still, many felt it unbelievable that such horrors could actually occur in a civilized society. Dutch historian Louis de Jong articulated what the civilized world felt about what was taking place:

> Here we approach an aspect of the Holocaust which is of cardinal importance and which can never be sufficiently underlined. That the Holocaust, when it took place, was beyond the belief and the comprehension of almost all people living at the time, Jews included. Everyone knew

that human history had been scarred by endless cruelties. But that thousands, nay millions of human beings – men, women, and children, the old and the young, the healthy and the infirm – would be killed, finished off, mechanically, industrially so to speak, would be exterminated like vermin – that was a notion so alien to the human mind, an event so gruesome, so new, that the instinctive, indeed the natural, reaction of most people was: it can't be true. (1)

What could be done. . .

CLM: Was there ever a point when there was a general sense of chaos throughout Holland?

RMD: When the Jewish laws became too big, there was chaos. The members of certain unions and work groups started a strike throughout Holland. Not the Jewish ones, but the other people, and that is when chaos actually came about; the beginning of unifying against, came about. And then the Germans started shooting groups of people which they discovered, as groups, and setting examples for people not to do that again. These were people who were working against German orders, resistance groups. They were intellectual people who tried to find ways to end it before it started. And they were shot down at certain places which were known to be the spots where people were executed. The Nazis came to people's homes and took them away in trucks and then sealed off the houses. But what could the people do? What can you do when you're so intimidated by everything going on around you? The only thing you could do was arrange to go into hiding. And many people did that, with business associates or other people they knew. But there was not much you could do beyond the rules that were set. And in Holland when they first put out the orders that Jews could not go to stores at certain times and Jews had to start wearing the star, that was when the labor strike started.

I think the Jewish people, most of them, still
had the hope that this was not going to last long.
That the war would soon end, and if it didn't that
it wouldn't last so long and we would come back. It
was really something you were not prepared to
think about. Because you didn't believe it, you
couldn't imagine that something that bad could
happen. You were so caught in the system that you
didn't know a way out to do it different – only the
ones who were prepared for it by having found
people willing to give them papers and hiding
places and who had financial possibilities. Which I
never thought about – I never thought, "Who's
going to pay for this?"

SLW: So some of them cooperated and others rebelled
(took a stand)?

RMD: First of all, your first rebellion was trying to get
papers without the J, from friends or acquaintances.
Then, when the time came, you went into hiding,
but not everybody could do that either. I think there
were a lot of babies and young kids brought into
safety by having them live with other people, non-
Jewish people, which (at the end of the war)
brought some problems with the few returning Jews
who had a right to their children.

So it was a very strange situation. If you
look at it, it's unbelievable that it could be so bad.
There's no resemblance to it somehow. And besides
that, the nonbelieving, that it could be so bad, that
they could do so many bad things, brought you to
surrender. It is ridiculous to think of ordering

groups of people to go to a certain spot, and voluntarily going to that spot. It's unbelievable.

SLW: Did your parents and brother have the same kind of attitude that you did?

RMD: Yeah, my father did. Because he was not really willing to surrender so easily.

SLW: But your mother was different?

RMD: She was such a good soul, that she didn't doubt anything. She lived in a sort of a dream world. She was very worried all the time, that was one thing about her. When my father and I came to visit her on her birthday, the last time, all she did was worry about how dangerous it was for us to come and visit her. And she was always looking after everyone. It drove us nuts by too much mothering; too much love. You couldn't take it. And that's why I say my brother paid a high price for surviving, by having to live with my mother for two years. And not being able to get away from her for a minute.

Margot,

You did so good speaking yesterday. I loved it. I learned so much and it was really interesting. I really liked how you talked about everything. You still seem to have no hate in your heart. I also liked how you seem to still find it in you to talk about it; all the bad. That's one thing I cannot do. When bad things have happened, I can't talk about them. You gave me courage and hope that someday I will be able to. Thanks so much.

Angie

Margot' mother, Erna, Bubi (Manfred) and Margot at a park in Berlin

Margot' mother, Erna, Bubi (Manfred) and Margot at a park in Berlin

Margot and brother, Manfred in
Berlin Circa 1931

Erna

Margot, Sweet 16, in
Holland 1937

Margot, in Holland 1938

Margot and Lo in yard of summer villa of the Meyers in Zandfoord (Netherlands)

Lodewyk, in Holland
1941

Original with J

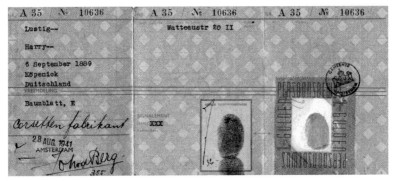

Back of Harry Lustig's original ID card

53

Harry's false ID without
the J

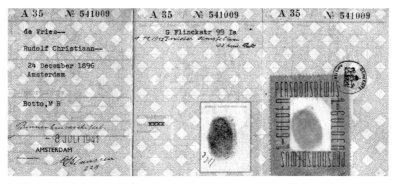

Back of Father's without the J

False ID for Erna

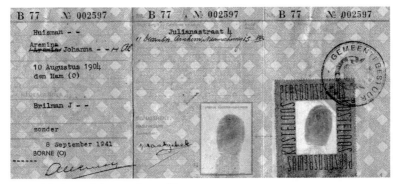

Erna's false ID card she was given a fake name

55

Margot's Father, Harry
Lustig

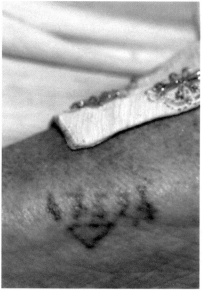

The tattoo Margot was
given at Auschwitz,
47574 above a triangle

Margot and Rudy DeWilde, 1997

Chapter 5

Attempted Escape to Switzerland

Margot could have gone into hiding for the duration of the war, just as her brother and parents did. This involved great danger, but her family decided that the risk of being deported to an unknown location and not knowing what they would be subjugated to, was even more perilous. While Margot's parents and brother had been fortunate enough to find safe hiding places, she and her in-laws decided they would try to flee from the persecution taking place in Holland. Margot thought that by remaining with Lo and his family, they could safely leave the German-occupied country and flee to someplace neutral. Margot's brothers-in-law negotiated plans to relocate them safely to Switzerland. They had a bank account there from which they withdrew money in the attempt to bribe their way out. A pay-out was arranged with a Swiss contact and a high-ranking German official. Margot, her husband and her in-laws were to take a train to Switzerland where they hoped to live in safety until the end of the war.

Lo's oldest brother, Philip, had a non-Jewish wife and newborn baby. They received news in March, 1943, that the family could escape to Switzerland on a certain day. They were informed that the sister-in-law and the baby could not take the train with them because it would be "too tiresome a trip." They later realized this should have been a red flag for them, but they were so fixated on leaving the country that nobody paid attention .

The family was told to present themselves at the central railway station in Amsterdam to take the express train to Switzerland. Margot's father came to the railway station and watched their departure from a distance. Lo was dressed in what Margot thought was a very curious way. He wore many layers of clothing: knickers, sports stockings, boots, shirt, sport jacket and a rain coat. Margot asked him, "Aren't you dressed funny for this trip?"

His answer was, "You never know what will happen."

Margot, Flora, Lo and his brothers were led to a train compartment reserved for them. There was another Jewish family in that compartment, who was also able to pay for passage out of Holland. The father was a diamond trader, with a wife and daughter about Margot's age. The German conductor who greeted them was dressed in civilian clothing, not in uniform. He kept an eye on them and told them that at the next station, which was the first stop in Germany, they would have to exit the train to get Swiss visas to carry with their passports. This was also a big, red flag which nobody noticed.

As soon as they stepped off the train in Cologne, both families were arrested by the Gestapo and taken to headquarters. They were accused of attempting to smuggle valuables out of the country. They were interrogated for days to find where they hid their money. Of course, they were not trying to smuggle anything. The interrogation proved futile.

The day of their capture, March 21, 1943, signified the beginning of the worst period of Margot's life. She was hoping for freedom. She had risked her life every time she left home carrying false papers. She expected this way of life would soon be over. It was an extremely stressful time, not knowing what would happen next. Every day, she wondered when she and her in-laws would be selected for deportation. They tried not to think about what might happen if they should all be taken away, for fear the rumors they occasionally heard might be true. She was relieved her parents and brother were safe and she still thought she and Lo could start a new life in Switzerland, where they could live in freedom. At some point, though, Philip's contact betrayed them. He turned them in and their hopes of escape were suddenly crushed. This was a heartbreaking blow to Margot and her in-laws. Suddenly, they had no idea what lay ahead. They felt powerless at that point to control their destinies and were at the mercy of the Nazis.

After three days in Cologne, they were forcibly escorted to a train along with the family who was captured with them and several other Jews, who were taken at a raid in Cologne. They were all sent to Berlin, the headquarters of deportation. They were taken to what was formerly a boys' school and kept there under SS supervision. The prisoners were put into classrooms, with straw on the floor for bedding.

Soon after arriving, Margot heard about a man working at the school. He was the brother of her mother's best girlfriend, Ernie Reschke, with whom she was a friend and schoolmate since the age of five. Ernie's brother, Max, had been the principal of the school, and was made the leader of this collection camp. Margot went down to the office to find Max and introduce herself. He fell off his chair in surprise, asking, "What are you doing here?!" Unfortunately, he was not able to help them. He had been forced to send his own mother on a transport just a week before. His sister, Ernie, also in Berlin, sometimes worked with him in the camp as a secretary. She visited Margot a couple of times and brought her a few pieces of food.

During her brief stay at the former school, Margot and Lo heard a call one day, "Dutch people! Dutch people!" They followed the voice and found a Dutch truck driver, who had heard they were taken prisoner. He gave them his address and said that if they were able to escape, he would help them further. He told them to write letters to whomever they wanted and he would deliver them, which he did. But that was all he could do while they were detained there. Margot gave him a letter for her father's contact. The letter told her father about what was happening. She told him to warn other people; which he did.

This all happened without them knowing the full truth about what was taking place. They only heard the occasional rumor and did not know what to believe. They could not imagine the kind of destruction that had been occurring. The previous year, 1942, was the most lethal year in Jewish history: 2.7 million Jews, along with countless other "undesirables," had lost their lives at the hands of Nazis.(2) Hitler's minions had been sweeping their way across Europe, gathering Jews and deporting them to labor and concentration camps as they went. They heard rumors that some families were allowed to remain together. They hoped to build a future someplace in the east, such as Poland or Russia. "Maybe it's not going to be so bad, so let's try to stay together," they reasoned. The Germans went to great lengths to hide the truth about where so many people selected for deportation were actually going. Besides requiring them to bring one suitcase with them, they sometimes provided warm clothing and food. So Margot and her in-laws did not try to escape from the school where they were being held prisoner. They knew enough about what was going on to realize that those who attempted escape and were caught were immediately shot.

After a few days of confinement in the school, Margot developed a sore throat and went to see the nurse who was working there. The nurse, after examining Margot, told her, "Scarlet fever. You must be quarantined." At this point, Margot does not recall saying good-bye to Lo, Flora and her brothers-in-law. She does not remember many details of that period, no doubt due to the fever she endured. She tried to get help from a doctor with the same last name as hers (her maiden name), and when she introduced herself to him, he did not want anything to do with her. But there was another doctor who told her he would take her to the hospital. His name was Dr. Ehrlich, which translated means "Dr. Honest." He proved to be a kind and honest doctor.

Dr. Ehrlich took Margot to the Jewish hospital where she was in the isolation ward with a White Russian woman who was also sick. The White Russians were not yet persecuted by the Germans; they were still colleagues-in-arms. This young woman was still free. Her mother and sister often visited her at the hospital. They took letters from Margot to the in-between address in Amsterdam to be delivered to her father. He received the letters and in response sent money, food and letters back to Margot. It was important that Margot be very discreet about what she wrote to her father, just in case the letters were confiscated and read. She did not want to cause her new friends any trouble.

Besides the food sent by her father, a Swiss aunt of Margot's also managed to have a food package sent to the camp while she was in the hospital. Upon recovery, she was released from quarantine, and escorted back to the holding camp.

Lo was still at the camp. Flora and Lo's brothers had already been sent away on separate transports. Both Margot and Lo had no idea where they had been taken. Ironically, her husband was allowed to stay and wait for her, so they could go together to Auschwitz. This added to their hope that maybe they would be relocated somewhere else and could start a new life.

As a Nonconformist. . .

CLM: The Meyers decided to try to leave the Netherlands. When you heard about the bombing of Pearl Harbor, what was your reaction to that?

RMD: Holland was neutral in both wars in the beginning and associated more with the United States than any other country. And when the war started, people began boycotting everything German. I did not know that they (Lo's family) had applied for emigration, but I learned that they had the papers for emigration on the day that Pearl Harbor was bombed. This meant that they had part of their fortune in another country; otherwise they wouldn't have had the chance to leave. So that was one thing which you took automatically. I don't know why I was so superficial, to go from one situation to the other without any problems.

SLW: Do you think people should have tried to stop the tyranny caused by the Nazis? Should the United States have been involved in the war earlier and done something about Hitler?

RMD: Yes. I think in the beginning America should have opened the gates for people to come in. It is a country which exists of people who came from someplace else. So when the necessity came about that some injustice was being done, they should have opened the doors and given the affected people a chance to escape. That would have been a good beginning. It's bad that so many people had to die for it.

SLW: It sounds like when you took the train out of Holland with Lo's family, he was expecting that something unexpected might happen. Did you have any doubts or fears that the trip might not go as planned? Were you very surprised when you were arrested?

RMD: I didn't have any idea that this could be a scam. I thought that we had bought our freedom. I think Lo had an inkling of something. Because I asked if he wasn't a little overdressed for going on a train ride. And he said the words, "You never know..." I think we were too trusting in many ways.

CLM: Do you remember what happened during the interrogation? Were you treated poorly?

RMD: They tried to find out where we hid the valuables. But they didn't have to find that out because the Swiss guy who handled the whole thing knew. So it was more pestering than anything else. But there was another family with us, in the same compartment, and from them they tried to find out where it was. We weren't even allowed to have any jewelry. I hid my ring in my curled up hair. I can't imagine how masses of people, thousands, ten thousands, hundred thousands of people were simply following orders. It didn't even come up in your mind to think something must be done about this. You went into hiding if you had the chance and otherwise you trusted that maybe it is not going to be so bad, maybe they will send us someplace where we can build a new future. They don't want us so they sent us out of the surroundings. That was really the idea that you were not only thinking about but automatically you assumed. And all those hundreds of thousands of people assumed.

Dear Margot,

After hearing how you suffered in your life, it truly helps to put things in perspective. It causes us to be aware of how much we have to be thankful for — mostly freedom. It is often hard to make history come alive. It is something of the past that we cannot easily comprehend. But hearing your story and seeing you sitting there helped me to realize that these are not just tragic stories we read, but rather true events which change the lives of millions, mostly in a negative way. Thank you for being willing to share with us how history has shaped your life. I can't imagine how awful it was for you. I admire your strength that brought you through. Thank you again.

Paula

Chapter 6
Arrival in Auschwitz

In June, 1943, a few days after Margot was released
from the hospital and the next transport was ready, she and
Lo, along with many others who had been detained at the
holding camp, were ordered onto a train. The boxcar had
a large sliding door with a bar on the outside. She learned
later that this was the second to last transport to leave
Berlin. It was very cramped, as there were many people
forced into each boxcar. There were some slits between the
boards of the walls. Prisoners inside could peek through
and get a glimpse of where they were going. Margot was
placed where she was not able to look out, though. She
travelled in the stifling train with no idea she was being
taken to Auschwitz.

The train rolled out of Germany and into Poland,
to a prison camp which Himmler had decided in 1940 to
construct for the purpose of establishing Nazi law and order
in the east. He had chosen this location at the foothills of
the Carpathians because it was fairly isolated yet had good
railroad connections. When Himmler first found it, there
were about twenty formerly Polish artillery barracks there.
At that time, they were virtually useless. The water supply
was polluted and the land marshy. Nonetheless, Himmler
chose SS Major Rudolf Hoess to organize the camp. Hoess
was confident that he could turn this area into a functioning
outpost for the Reich. The Poles had named this place
Oswiecim; the Germans referred to it as Auschwitz. It

was Hoess who apparently designed the famous steel sign that hung above the gate to Auschwitz: Arbeit Macht Frei ("Work makes you free"), which mocked and offered false promise to arriving prisoners. Hoess had begun organizing the camp by rounding up local Polish Jews and political prisoners. The prisoners were forced to live in the existing barracks while they constructed/restored the rest of the camp. At first, Auschwitz was intended to be a detention camp that would confine dissidents. The Nazis wanted to build an Aryan nation and prevent the new order from being infected by association with non-Aryans.

Once Himmler realized the value of the free labor at his disposal, his plans became more grandiose. He decided Auschwitz would become an agricultural research station. Also, factories could be built nearby to make truck tires and other supplies for the war effort. The slave labor used for these factories was housed at the camp. The prisoners were entirely expendable; they were worked to death and continually replaced.

In 1941, Himmler decided Auschwitz should become more productive. He told Hoess the camp would house not only the 10,000 to 50,000 prisoners that had been previously agreed upon, but would expand to accommodate 100,000 prisoners. Hoess was ordered to build an additional camp, Auschwitz II, in the woods near what had once been the village of Brzezinka. The addition was two miles west of Auschwitz. The Germans called this expansion area Birkenau. A third camp, Auschwitz III, was eventually built near the village of Monowice and was called Monowitz-Buna. The I.G. Farben Company used thousands of prisoners in this camp to labor in its synthetic rubber plant. The company was ultimately unsuccessful at its production of rubber products. Many other manufacturers also took advantage of the free labor to produce German war products.

As Hitler's armies swept across Russia, thousands of Russians were taken captive and sent to Auschwitz and other camps. They were used as laborers for building the Birkenau prisoner-of-war camp. These prisoners were also treated as completely expendable. Many died from exhaustion and starvation. Within a year, most of the remaining Russian prisoners were shot in a copse near Birkenau and buried in a massive pit. Later that year, because of ground water poisoning and the stench of decomposing bodies, the corpses were exhumed and burned.

In the summer of 1941, Himmler sent Hoess to attend a secret meeting in Berlin. There he was informed by Himmler that "the Fuhrer has ordered that the Jewish question be solved once and for all, and that we, the SS, are to implement that order." (3) Himmler decided only Auschwitz was large enough and sufficiently isolated to serve this purpose. He put Hoess in charge of this onerous task, and sent Major Adolf Eichmann, head of the Reich Security Office (RSHA), to help work out the details. Together, they planned the geographic shipments of Jews to Auschwitz and devised efficient methods of mass exterminations. They agreed poisonous gas was the most practical method. Hoess was given the task of finding a more expedient method than piping exhaust fumes into truck beds, as was already being done by the Einsatzgruppen.

In September, 1941, Hoess was away on business. Deputy Commandant Karl Fritzsch decided to experiment with Zyklon B, a commercial form of hydrocyanic acid which was activated by contact with air. So far, it had been used for vermin control, which was its designed purpose. Fritzsch killed 600 Russian prisoners of war and 250 tubercular patients by sealing them into underground bunkers and releasing Zyklon B into their midst. Thus, he discovered the method Hoess and Eichmann considered "suitable" for mass exterminations.

By 1942, Auschwitz had become the largest concentration and death camp of the Third Reich. Barracks and crematoria were erected. The rounding up and transporting of Jews to Auschwitz from all over Germany and the other occupied countries had begun. The first mass gassings began. News arrived from Berlin that Birkenau was to house not 100,000 prisoners but 200,000. It became the center for the "Final Solution." Thousands of Jews and other "undesirables" were brought daily for extermination. Those who were kept alive were used either as slave labor or as subjects of experiments.

By the time Margot and Lo arrived at Auschwitz, it was a fully functioning *Vernichtung* (extermination camp). Normally it would have been about a six hour train ride from the holding camp in Berlin where they had been detained, to Auschwitz. In their case it took an entire day, and they did not arrive until the next morning. The train had to stop several times on side tracks to let priority transportation (military troop trains) pass. During that long train ride, some people became sick; some died. No food or water was provided for the prisoners during the transport. They were packed together tightly, with hardly any room to sit or move.

When the train arrived at Auschwitz, Margot heard

the bar as it was removed from the boxcar. The sliding
door opened, along with much yelling and screaming at
the newly-arrived prisoners. Everyone was ordered out.
On the platform stood people in blue and white striped
uniforms who were commandeering everyone. These were
the *Kapos*, the prisoners who acted as trusties to carry out
the orders of the SS. They had to do their jobs thoroughly,
better even than the Germans, if they hoped to stay alive.
They had to organize and "process" the newly arrived
prisoners.

The smell of Auschwitz was overpowering.
A terrible, burning smell permeated the air. Four
new crematoria were operating at Birkenau and one
at Auschwitz. About 180 prisoners worked at each
crematorium to keep the extermination process moving
efficiently. At that time, the crematoria at Birkenau burned
thousands of corpses a day. The fires burned day and night.

After the prisoners were off the train, they were
divided into groups by two SS officers. One of the officers
was the infamous Dr. Josef Mengele, known as the Angel
of Death. Mothers with children formed one line; women
without children another; men formed a different line and
old people formed the fourth group. The officers then
assessed each prisoner and waved him or her in a different
direction. Although most of the incoming prisoners did
not realize it at the time, a wave to the right meant survival
for the time being. Most of these were assigned to a
labor *Kommando*, hard labor for those who looked young
and fit enough. Others were waved to the left and never
seen again. They were immediately sent to their deaths.
Anyone who looked more than about forty years of age,
most women and almost all children were sent to the left.

The whole process of sorting people was referred to as "*selektion*." Margot later learned that there were many factories nearby, where the Jewish prisoners who were selected to go to the right were worked to death for the Nazis.

Dr. Josef Mengele conducted the *selektion* on the day Margot arrived at Auschwitz. After Margot, Lo and the others were separated into groups, Mengele commanded that young, married women step forward. Margot was a young, married woman, so she stepped forward. About twenty-five other women were in the same group. They were taken in a truck to a shower room. Margot and some of the other women were very nervous. She had heard rumors in Holland that this shower room may actually be a gas room. The first thing Margot did when she entered was to look for valves. She expected that if it was a gas chamber, there would be valves somewhere on the walls. There were none. Later, she learned that there would not have been valves at all, because the poison was dropped into the gas chambers through ceiling vents.

The women were, in fact, taken to a normal shower room. They endured the humiliation of having their hair shaved and their clothing taken away. It became difficult to distinguish who was who anymore. Then they were given clothing which had been confiscated from earlier prisoners. After a cold shower, they were loaded onto a truck again and taken to a series of brick buildings. Margot later learned these were the original soldiers' quarters before the camps were built. Margot and the other women were assigned to live in Block 10, one of the old barracks at the original Auschwitz rather than across the railroad tracks at Birkenau. People who were selected to work in factories in the area were housed in very primitive buildings in Birkenau and fed for as long as they were able to work. Margot's barrack was brick, rather than the wood and plywood barracks of Birkenau. The brick barracks provided slightly better shelter.

The women had no idea what was going to happen next. There were already prisoners in the barrack who had arrived on previous transports from Belgium, France and Czechoslovakia. The Czechs had arrived at Auschwitz before the others, so they were given the preferred "positions" (job assignments). These previously selected women were the leaders of the block and the so-called nurses of the hospital and experimentation rooms. There were two lawyers' wives who were Polish who were the supervisors of the sick room. Some of the Czech prisoners acted as doctors' assistants for the experiments, although they were not qualified as doctors. The new arrivals quickly learned the rules and politics of Block 10.

Soon after being taken to the barrack, some "artists" arrived who tattooed numbers and triangles on the prisoners' forearms. As soon as Margot had her number, 47574, tattooed on her arm, she went to a washroom with a clay floor. She rubbed her arm with the coarse clay in an attempt to erase the tattoo. She managed to partially remove it, so that it was no longer legible. She was soon caught and tattooed again.

Margot and all other prisoners who arrived at Auschwitz and survived the *selektion* were no longer treated as human beings, but as numbers. The same numbers that were tattooed on their arms when they first arrived, along with their identifying triangle, had to be sewn onto their clothing. The triangles identified, by the color and position of the point, the group to which each prisoner belonged. The Jewish prisoners were identified by a red triangle pointed down. The German political prisoners were identified by a red triangle pointed up. The Jehovah's Witnesses were marked with a purple color; green was for criminals; pink for homosexuals; etc. Each prisoner was assigned a triangle which visually identified him or her. In the barrack where Margot was relegated, all the women were Jewish. Therefore, they each had a red triangle on their clothing below their numbers.

Margot and the other prisoners were awakened early every morning, not very pleasantly, while it was still dark. They were forced to stand in counting lines for *"appell"* (roll call). This generally occurred inside on the lower level of the barrack. Their numbers were called and they had to answer, "Present." Occasionally, the counting took place outside. These daily sessions sometimes lasted for hours. At counting sessions in other barracks, if anyone did not look healthy or strong enough, they were sent to the trucks, and that meant the gas chamber. The prisoners who were gassed as soon as they arrived at Auschwitz were considered by some to be better off, because they did not know ahead of time what was going to happen to them. The prisoners later learned that gassing took place inside the buildings that had long underground structures with pillars to hold up the tops. There were some benches around the pillars and walls. Margot learned that people who were meant to be gassed were brought into these big rooms for their so-called "shower" and forced to undress. Then they were led into what looked like a large shower room. The guards locked the doors and windows from the outside. The Germans then dumped canisters of poison

(Zyklon B), which looked like over-sized paint cans, down the chimney. Most people did not stay alive for long. Others endured a longer fight until they finally succumbed, too. From there, they were hauled to the crematoria next door and burned.

After the daily morning counting sessions, Margot and the other prisoners in her barrack were given a scoopful of unidentifiable brown liquid. It was intended to resemble coffee or tea, but the only similarities were its color and temperature. It was the only liquid they received each day. It had to be boiled because the water supply at the camp was tainted with cholera and other contaminants.

After receiving their drinks, everyone dispersed to her part of the barrack. Downstairs were the experimentation, administrative, and two sick rooms. The upstairs was divided into two sides. A brick stove and bunk beds were on each side. The stoves were attached to the floor. Each had a big opening for heating material and a chimney. The areas near the stoves were occupied by the privileged, early arrivals in the camp. They were in charge of ensuring that the rooms remained clean. Bunks were stacked three-high. Each prisoner was issued a straw mattress pad, straw pillow and a woolen horse blanket. Most bunks did not have enough support boards. Every morning, the prisoners meticulously made their bunks before inspection. The women kept their few possessions hidden inside their beds. These items usually were stolen from someone else. If, upon inspection, one's bed was improperly made, punishment was administered. Next, the prisoners did whatever tasks they were assigned for the day. Many days, there was nothing to do. Occasionally, some of the prisoners were sent on a *Kommando*, which would take them outside the camp.

The big, brick square stoves in the building had tiles around them, in which the fires were kept burning. If a prisoner was able to "organize" (steal) something edible on a *Kommando* and wanted it cooked, she gave it to the woman in charge of the stove who then cooked it in exchange for a portion of the food. These women were considered the "queens" of the area, because all the women in the barrack depended on them. They were also in charge of the barrels of liquid food that were delivered daily to Block 10 to be distributed.

The main meal was at noontime. Some of the women in charge of the food dished out the soup downstairs from the vats which were delivered. Each prisoner was issued a galvanized food bowl. It was a good idea to be on friendly terms with the woman who served the soup, in order to be given a scoop from the bottom of the barrel. If the server did not like someone, that person would not receive as much solid food. This meant that she took a scoop of brew from the top of the vat instead of the bottom where the chunks had settled. Margot was not friends with the Polish woman who was usually in charge of the food, but she was not on negative terms with her, either. She received scoops mostly from near the bottom of the vat.

When Margot first arrived at Auschwitz, she had a strange feeling of déjà vu. Of course, she never had been there before, nor had she ever been in Poland. But she learned that her great grandfather had come from that region. She attributed the feelings of familiarity to these ancestral roots. Thus began Margot's imprisonment in Auschwitz, which was to last over two long years.

First days at Auschwitz. . .

SLW: Had you heard about the gassings at concentration camps before arriving at Auschwitz?

RMD: A little bit. But we didn't know everything. We heard rumors of the concentration camps and the gas. That's why I looked around to see a valve first when I came into the building. It was really not something that was proven yet. Some people believed the stories. The story was that they didn't want the Jews around and they would take them and bring the families together in another country so they could start a new life. That was the beginning. And many people believed it. My father so believed in everything, wishful thinking, and his actions followed. Everyone was ordered to apply for emigration by filling out a form, answering all kinds of questions. By doing so, you let them know exactly what you owned and what possessions you had. Because they asked what you have and what you would like to take along, and so on. So they took that information and used it for other purposes. No, that was very ignorant of people. They did not foresee it. And we still believed in the fact of being condemned to live someplace else, but we thought, "Well, when the war is over everything will be okay again."

CLM: At the time you were brought to Block 10, did you feel as though you and the other women were somehow different than the majority of prisoners at Auschwitz?

RMD: Yes, in our case I was very much aware that we were an exception to something. We didn't know what we were there for yet, but you realized this was something different.

CLM: What made you realize that?

RMD: I don't know – instinct or atmosphere. You knew that the ones who were commandeering you around were also prisoners who had come earlier. And the survivors of the earlier group had all the positions. By having a position, they had more of a chance to lead a normal life. So, that you could see. But still I realized that we were in a more favored situation than the prisoners outside Block 10. Because we were in a group of women who were ordered to step forward, if you were a young, married woman. So it was a distinction, a difference.

SLW: When the number 47574 was tattooed on your arm at Auschwitz, you tried to remove it. Since the war, do you have a different feeling about the number?

RMD: It's a tattoo which shows I survived. It's an honor mark for me. A lot of people had theirs removed, they didn't want it. For me, I deserved it. It shows I have been there.

SLW: What was the worst part of being at Auschwitz?

RMD: The worst things I remember were not knowing

what you were there for, from minute to minute and not knowing how long it would last. But as I was a fatalist, I trusted that this had a reason. I think I was always like this, that whatever has to happen will happen anyway.

CLM: Was Lo also fatalistic?

RMD: No, he was a strictly religious person who lived with indifference to the war, because his idealism was so big that it took completely over. Lo obeyed rules given 5000 years ago and longer. He believed God was with us so we would soon continue our plans to settle in Palestine.

Dear Margot DeWilde,
Thank you so much for coming to our school and talking to us. I thought it was so interesting that you said when you reached the concentration camp, that you felt that you had been there before or that you thought that your ancestors had been there before. Thank you so much for sharing your experiences with us.

Mary

Chapter 7
Medical Experimentation Block

Soon after being quartered in Block 10, Margot recognized a woman named Ima, who was already at the camp. They had taken dance lessons together in Holland. Ima recognized Margot right away. They each enjoyed a sense of relief at finding a familiar face. After this brief reprieve, she informed Margot of what was actually taking place at Auschwitz, confirming the rumors about the gassing and cremating. Margot became worried about what might have happened to Lo. She did not know if he had been sent to the gas chamber on the day of their arrival. Margot fervently hoped that he had been selected for some type of labor.

Ima told Margot about the various positions that were assigned to the women in Block 10. These women were fortunate to be assigned positions. These positions provided them with some security. If one had a job and performed it well, this provided the possibility of delaying or preventing a worse fate. Already, Ima had been assigned a function in Block 10. In her civilian life she was married to a doctor and her father was a doctor. Therefore, because of this association, she was given the function of nurse in one of the sickrooms in the barrack. Although the sickrooms were not equipped to provide adequate nursing care, this position provided Ima with a semblance of security.

Margot learned from Ima the reason she and the

other women had been singled out during the *selektion*.
They would be used as subjects in human experiments.
The Block 10 barrack where she was assigned was actually
a medical experimentation block. Eventually, most of
the women were used as research subjects. The women,
however, were not aware of the purpose or nature of the
tests being conducted.

Besides Dr. Mengele, several other doctors worked
at Auschwitz. The chief physician of the camp, Dr. Eduard
Wirths, appointed Mengele as the senior doctor in the
women's camp at Birkenau. Besides his diabolic duty
of *selektion*, Mengele supervised and performed many
horrific experiments on prisoners, especially twins, for
various studies. Mengele also performed a different type
of *selektion*, which involved sorting prisoners from the sick
bays whom he felt were too ill to work. These prisoners
were taken to the gas chamber. After the *selektion* at her
arrival in Auschwitz, she did not see him again. She was
kept alive for a different fate in the experimentation block
of the original Auschwitz.

The Nazis were attempting to find a way to
eliminate the propagation of all unwanted races and
religions in Europe. Hitler had imagined himself becoming
ruler of the entire continent. To this end, he wanted to get
rid of the "undesirables" in order to lead a pure Aryan race
of people. But instead of eliminating all "undesirables,"
they planned to sterilize all non-Aryans who were kept
alive for slave labor or other purposes. Later, Margot
learned that she and the other women in Block 10 were
slated for sterilization experiments.

The Nazis' goal was to develop a method of mass
sterilization that was both quick and inexpensive. This was

important to Himmler's racial theory. Careful attention and time were devoted to the experiments. Surgical methods of sterilization were already known. Those were considered too slow and expensive, so the Nazis experimented with chemicals and radiation. Himmler found a professor at the University of Konigsberg, Dr. Carl Clauberg, who ran a treatment center for sterile women. He felt that Clauberg was qualified to turn his expertise in the opposite direction to develop a method of mass sterilization. Clauberg eagerly accepted Himmler's invitation to gain official backing for his research and a steady supply of research subjects. (3, pg. 57-58)

When Margot arrived at Auschwitz, Dr. Clauberg had only been there a short while and was beginning his research. There were over two hundred women at his disposal in Block 10, which became known as "Clauberg's Block" (2). Each woman was summoned downstairs to one of the experimentation rooms. Two Czechoslovakian women had been assigned to assist Dr. Clauberg. He experimented with various chemical formulas that he injected into the women's cervixes for the purpose of obstructing the fallopian tubes. The ingredients of these concoctions were kept secret, but the main ingredient was a solution of formalin (3, pg.58). After receiving treatments, x-rays were taken. Three weeks later, each woman was x-rayed again. These were compared to assess the effectiveness of the treatments.

A Dutch transport arrived, which brought scarlet fever and diphtheria to Block 10. A sick room downstairs was made into an isolation room. This was done secretly, because if the Nazis in charge found out about the infectious diseases, everyone in the barrack would have been sent to the gas chambers. The Nazis did not want any prisoners to die of natural causes or diseases; they preferred to do the killing themselves. The Polish Jewish doctor, who was in charge of the barrack, kept the diseases undercover. She quarantined the prisoners as much as possible. She wanted somebody who previously had scarlet fever to care for the quarantined prisoners. Margot volunteered for this duty. She thought she was immune based on her belief that she had scarlet fever in Berlin. She had been misdiagnosed, though, and had actually contracted a different sickness - which she thinks was probably strep throat.

As time passed, Margot continued her work in the isolation room as a nurse's assistant. She emptied bedpans, kept the place clean, and performed a variety of other tasks. When a patient became dehydrated, the only treatment available involved attaching a hose and needle to a large syringe. This device was used to press saline solution into the upper leg, while another person massaged the liquid into the patient's tissue. It eventually became Margot's responsibility to administer the shots. Sometimes, she was awakened during the night to perform this duty. She was not required to do this very often, though, because the amount of saline solution supplied to the sick room was extremely low.

Margot eventually became infected with scarlet fever. She had the nervous habit of biting her nails, and assumes she contracted the virus that way. She became extremely sick. The Polish doctor liked Margot and gave her one injection, a forerunner of penicillin, to combat her sickness. Margot was conscious of receiving the shot, but remembers little else from the time of her illness. She was told after her recovery that she was semi-conscious for twelve days. She eventually regained enough of her strength to continue her duties. Later, she became sick again. This time she had rheumatic fever. Her throat became very swollen so she often held it open with a toothbrush in order to breath.

The prisoners in Block 10, who were fortunate enough to have been assigned positions, were sometimes exempt from experiments. Margot had been given the function of pot-carrier for the quarantine room. This enabled her to temporarily avoid being called for experimentation. But, eventually, she was told, "Position or not, you have to come down." She reported to the experimentation room and received a treatment. Margot and the other women who were subjected to this humiliating procedure did not know the purpose of the injections. They speculated that it may be sterilization or insemination. The women returned upstairs afterward - some in pain; others not. Margot does not remember it as being particularly painful.

Sylvia Friedmann, a Czechoslovakian prisoner nurse, administered the injections and observed the women for symptoms of any kind. A few weeks after receiving their treatment, the women were required to report downstairs again and were x-rayed to determine whether or not the treatment produced the desired result. After the war, they learned that the procedure was indeed sterilization.

Some prisoners feared being sent to Birkenau, which meant the likelihood of perishing in the gas chambers. They considered Block 10 as "a piece of luck and the possibility of survival." Clauberg encouraged some

"patients" to have faith by telling them he was planning
". . . to take them to his private research clinic at
Konigshutte, just a few kilometers from Auschwitz." That
may have been true, because Hoess reported later that
". . . after the successful experiment, . . . Clauberg planned
that every one of the female prisoners at the end of a year
undergo sexual intercourse with a male prisoner chosen
especially for this purpose." The project included a plan
to test the success of Clauberg's sterilization procedures.
Most fortunately, though, this appalling test was never
performed ". . . because of the course of the war." (5)
Margot, and the other prisoners, were never informed of
these or any other future plans.

   After the war, Margot and the other prisoners of
Block 10 learned that they had been considered "bought
material." Because they were consigned to Dr. Clauberg,
they had the advantage of receiving slightly better
treatment than the inmates of Birkenau. They were not
used for hard labor and were allowed more free time. The
food rations were slightly larger and the women were
kept a little healthier, in order to be better subjects for the
experiments. Of course, Margot was unaware of these
details and only learned this later. She did not know at the
time the full extent of how miserable the conditions were at
Birkenau.

   Occasionally, Margot and the other women in
Block 10 were ordered outside without knowing the reason.
Usually, the building was cleared, sprayed and sterilized
against bedbugs and fleas. Each inmate was ordered to
shower, after which she received a clean set of clothing.
These clothes were recycled from incoming prisoners who
had been gassed.

Once, when Block 10 was infested with bedbugs, Ima gave Margot a white sheet to use for bedding. Margot considered this to be quite a luxury. The sheet provided a buffer between the horse blanket and the rough straw mattress on her bunk. She soon realized that using it for this purpose was futile, though, because when the lights were turned out at night, the bedbugs were attracted to the sheet. Margot sometimes gathered the sheet and took it to the hallway overlooking a guard who was sitting downstairs. She then quietly shook the sheet over the railing of the staircase, causing the bedbugs to rain down upon the guard. But more bedbugs inevitably infested her sheet, so Margot and some of the other inmates decided to use the fabric to make bras and aprons. The aprons were traded with the nurses in exchange for small portions of food.

Meanwhile, Margot's husband was still alive, although she was unaware of this. She had not seen Lo since they day they arrived at Auschwitz. Margot remained hopeful he had been selected for labor. (Note: It was not until 2008 that Margot found an official record that listed Lo as a prisoner taken to Buna.) One day, she was told by one of the male nurses from the sick barrack, Block 9, who delivered their food that Lo was next door. This person was a German prisoner who had been sent to Auschwitz for political crimes. Lo had been taken from another camp to the sick barrack in early 1944. She was told the Nazis worked people to near death and then sometimes took them to a sick barrack to recover, only to be returned to hard labor. When too many people arrived in the transports, the overflow prisoners were also put into the sick barracks until they could be gassed. At the time, Margot could not understand what was happening nor make sense of the system.

Margot gained contact with Block 9 through the person who informed her of Lo's arrival. Through this man, Margot was able to send short notes and food to Lo. Twice a week, Margot and the other prisoners received solid food, such as a piece of bread and something to go along with it. These food portions became quite undersized by the time they reached the intended prisoners, because the people handling the food each took a small piece. So by the time Margot received her allotment, she was able to send only a very meager portion to her husband. She was able to partially compensate for giving Lo her solid food by taking more soup when it was dished out, because it was her job to deliver soup to the patients in the isolation room. She survived many days on a diet of nothing but watery soup. Although it did not provide adequate nourishment, it was warm and filling.

During the short time that Lo was in the sick barrack, Margot was able to catch a glimpse of him once through the cracks of the boarded window of her barrack. The messenger had arranged to have Lo look out the window of the sick barrack at the same time. She saw an unfamiliar face with large ears and a shaved head. He had become very thin and did not look at all like he had when Margot had last seen him. Her first thought was, "Can I really be married to him?" It was a very strange feeling for her. She wondered if she could remain married to Lo, after what they had been through, if they both somehow managed to survive and be released someday. He gestured to Margot with his hands to ask her if she was pregnant, because he thought she may have been carrying their child.

She shook her head to indicate that she was not. This was the only time Margot saw Lo in Auschwitz since the day of their arrival and it was also the last; she never saw him again.

The messenger informed Margot in March, 1944, almost a year after her arrival, that her husband died in a bunk in Block 9. He had Jewish prayer boxes on his arms and forehead, which were commonly used in daily Jewish Orthodox tradition during prayers. Somebody had probably organized (stole) these for him. Before he died, Lo had been kept from *selektion* twice by a friend who wanted to do a favor for Margot. This friend used her influence with her boyfriend in the other block to keep Lo's name off the list of men to be sent to the gas chambers. Margot believes Lo died of tuberculosis in a bunk in Block 9.

Throughout Margot's imprisonment in Auschwitz, she occasionally saw prisoners come and go from Block 10. After she had been there awhile, an experiment was done with a dozen Greek prisoners. These beautiful, tanned women endured horrifying operations. Margot was told that their female organs had been surgically removed. Most, if not all, did not survive. Another time, Margot was told about an anthropological experiment that was conducted. The heads and bone structures of ten women from Block 10 were measured. This research was rumored to be led by a professor of anthropology. Margot and the other prisoners never saw them again nor heard what happened to them.

There was a mother and daughter from Cologne who refused to report when it was their turn for experiments. "We didn't see them again," said Margot.

However, Margot did not presume they were killed. She thought they had been assigned to a work detail.

Margot realized there were no guarantees in Auschwitz. She lived from one day to another, never sure of what would happen next. This was the hardest part of her imprisonment - not knowing what lay ahead for her. All her plans for the future died along with Lo.

About Block 10...

SLW: Did you ever find out where Lo had been sent to work while he was in Auschwitz?

RMD: According to some information that was sent to me recently through the Red Cross, Lo had been sent to labor in Buna before he became sick.

CLM: How did you feel when you saw Lo through the barred window of Block 10?

RMD: When I saw him in camp that time, my first instinct was, "Is that the man I would live my life with?" Somehow something very strange happened to me at that moment.

CLM: Did he seem like a stranger?

RMD: Not a stranger, but what you automatically thought at that time suddenly became doubtful. And I don't know why I had that crazy idea. I knew I would survive, I knew he wouldn't. I knew I would survive by myself. And that is plainly because I'm always against everything, what people expect me to do, so in this case they wanted to kill me and I wasn't going to be killed, if I could help it. Lo would fight for Palestine, the land of the free Jews, that was his ideal. But he was not a free spirit. He followed the rules which he had chosen to follow. And that's why I sometimes doubt, did he die in the bunk as they told me or did he go in the gas chamber? I had the idea that there was someone willing to keep him off that list for me. I was liked by people and when you had a position, so much more was possible. Not officially, but there was so much more to secretly be done. And I had the idea that one of the nurses whose praise I took, and who was friends with the head of the barrack where my husband was confined, had pleaded with him to keep Lo off the list.

SLW: What did you do for most of the day when you were not involved in your duties as pot carrier?

RMD: Just waiting for one minute to go by without something happening. That was the hardest thing – the uncertainty first, number one, and really not knowing what was going to happen in the next minute.

SLW: Was it the boredom?

RMD: No, I was not bored, because I always volunteered for groupings.

SLW: Why did you volunteer so often?

RMD: I thought whatever I do, as long as I get out of these walls for a few minutes or few hours, I'll volunteer. But I don't remember how often that happened. Because later, after the second Dutch transport, I volunteered for work in the quarantine room.

SLW: Where did everyone in the barracks think the mother and daughter from Cologne were taken? Did you assume they were taken to the gas chamber?

RMD: Not necessarily. They could have been taken to another camp, to do work duty. We didn't know what happened to them. And it was also something you could not imagine or think about because you didn't know. You couldn't presume anything because you didn't have an example. And that was the most distressing part, I think, for me, in that case. Not being in control. Others did with you what they wanted to do, and you were not in a position to do anything different. I could not imagine why everything went the way it went. There must have been really a mass hypnosis, for all the people in Europe, that they did not think any further than taking the facts. You can't imagine how it was otherwise possible. And after you were there for a time, you were so used to the daily run of life, if you could call it life, that you didn't even think about it. You just took it as a fact to go from one day into the other, hoping that you would see the end.

SLW: Were the women in the block generally somber or were there highs and lows?

RMD: Well, there were highs and lows in the people themselves and what they made out of their lives. Such as, we got together and we talked about books or theatre or whatever, and the other group talked about their plans to go to Israel, how their lives would be, so you had a few people who were psychologically alert.

SLW: Did they do a lot of reminiscing, about the good ol'

days?

RMD: Yes, there were reminiscences, especially in
       the beginning. Reminiscing and exaggerating the
       circumstances from before that time. Sharing
       recipes, cooking, was a very necessary part. You
       lost yourself into some sort of satisfaction, probably,
       from talking about it. And there was a lot of not
       thinking at all, for me. There must have been times
       that I really didn't think one step further than I did
       at that moment.

CLM: You didn't think about the past or the future, just the
       present?

RMD: Right, because if you would have thought about
       it too much you would be anxious to get out, and
       in this case you just took it for a fact to go from one
       day to the other, hoping that you would make it. I
       don't know how we ever got to that. You were
       planted in that building with no information,
       nothing, so your life was really, in the beginning,
       from minute to minute. You didn't know what was
       going to happen next.

CLM: Was there kind of a pecking order amongst the
women?

RMD: Yes, there was somewhat. The ones that had been
there for a longer time were more dominant than those
who had recently arrived. They were meaner than the ones
which came new.

Margot,

Thank you so much for coming in to talk to us yesterday. I found it interesting that you were able to get more soup to eat, while most were only given the minimum. It was great of you to give your solid food to Lo. Thanks again!

Rachel

Dear Margot,

Thank you so much for coming and telling us about your experience during the war. I had no idea that young, married women were separated. I also didn't know that you worked with the sick and were experimented on. I think it's great that you share your story with so many. Thanks again.

Ryan

Chapter 8
Life at Auschwitz

The prisoners faced constant, pervasive hunger
at Auschwitz. Upon arrival, they were already famished
because of the food shortages they had endured from
wherever they came - often a ghetto. During the long train
rides, they often went days without food or water. By the
time Margot and the other women who were selected were
finally housed in Block 10, they were all dehydrated and
hungry. They were not provided with an adequate amount
of food. Food became the dominant factor in the prisoners'
lives. They passed much of their time searching and
negotiating for more food as well as imagining, planning
and discussing new menus and recipes.

Most of the time at Auschwitz Margot was trapped
in Block 10. Despite the constant uncertainty of her fate,
life at the camp was monotonous. Margot volunteered for
work *kommandos* whenever she had a chance, because that
meant leaving the confining walls of the barrack. One time,
in the beginning of her imprisonment, she was assigned to
a work *kommando*. She and about a dozen other women
were sent outdoors. They were given baskets and led to a
hill. There, they were instructed to pick up rocks and carry
them to the other side of the hill. The next day, they picked
up the same rocks and returned them to their previous
location. Prison guards at Auschwitz were notorious for
assigning prisoners this kind of degrading, meaningless
work.

Sometimes, though, there were work *kommandos* which were beneficial. The groups (usually 10-15 prisoners) were always escorted by one or two soldiers and a guard dog. These men were often wounded soldiers from the front who were sent to concentration camps to act as guards during their recuperations. Some of them were decent men who did not know, before they arrived at Auschwitz, the horrors committed there. They had heard stories, but did not know the truth or extent of what was actually happening. They did not take part in the atrocities.

Once, Margot and a few other prisoners were led to a field where some plants were growing and the guard in charge said, "I'm going to smoke a cigarette." He then faced the other direction, taking a few steps away. This meant that they were allowed to go into the field and "organize" something edible. Similar situations occurred in which the guards who were leading the women in work *kommandos* gave implied permission for them to search the area for anything suitable to eat. Several times as they walked through nearby farm fields, the guard on duty would say something to the effect, "I'll turn around, but be quick." He would then look the other way as they stole produce such as carrots or rutabagas.

There was another memorable experience Margot had when she was sent with a group of women to pick mushrooms for the female guards in the barrack. The mushrooms grew in a meadow where they were fertilized by horse manure. They gathered the large, flavorless mushrooms for the guards. Then, while the guard who had led them there turned away, they quickly ate as many small ones as they could find. These young mushrooms were more flavorful and provided nutrition for the prisoners.

Margot learned to distinguish which plants were edible, such as herbs and wild greens. If she found anything that was safe to eat, she would gather it whenever given the chance. Margot and a few other women were once sent to gather acorns, which the Germans used to make foot baths for soldiers. They were able to sneak acorns into the barrack. The women had them fried on the stove even though they tasted terrible. Of course, they had to surrender a generous share to the woman who cooked them, but they each managed to get a few for themselves. By taking advantage of these opportunities to gain a little extra food, Margot and some of the other prisoners were able to supplement their meager diets.

One day, Margot and the others received a bowl of soup that "smelled very appetizing and tasted delectable." This was unusual, as the daily soup was typically tasteless. As she was eating, she found a small bone in the bowl. It looked like a small vertebrate. At first she had the horrifying thought that maybe it was part of a human finger. After rationalizing it, she realized that it must be a bone from the tail of an animal; most likely a pig.

Margot was once sent with two other women to a building where supplies were kept. Very little was ever dispensed to prisoners, but on this day they were instructed to get some items that Margot presumed were for medical experiments. When they arrived, an old German officer was on duty. He said to them, "Hello, girls. Did you have coffee?" They were taken aback by his kindness. They had almost forgotten what coffee tasted like! He filled a mug and handed it to the three of them to share. They each took a sip and immediately began gulping for air. It turned out to be crème de coco, which was very strong for them.

It was far richer than anything they had consumed in a long time. They found it to be absolutely incredible and relished every sip.

After finishing the drink, the officer said to them, "Take whatever you want, but don't let me see it." So Margot and the two women were allowed to gather some items which they took back to Block 10. They chose a few articles of clothing, because they had been issued only one set which they had to wear until the next time they were all taken outside during Block 10 lice fumigation. The supplies were in the district of the camp called "Canada." It was named after the country known to the Germans for its prosperity and abundance. The items accumulated in "Canada" had been taken from all of the prisoners who entered the camp. "Canada" stored clothing, utensils, blankets, luggage, medical supplies, etc.

It was difficult for the women in Block 10 to remain clean. They were allowed to shower only once every few weeks. They even had difficulty washing their hands because there were always 150 to 200 women living in the barrack at any given time and only a dozen faucets in the washroom. Horrifically, the soap issued to the prisoners was made from the ashes of the dead. The letters RIF (Ruhe in Friede; "rest in peace") were pressed into the gritty, gray bars.

Margot and the other women in Block 10 managed to maintain some of their cultural life. They gathered together sometimes to share their dreams of the future and to reflect on what their lives were like before imprisonment. These conversations were bittersweet, melancholy, hopeful and essential to their sanity. Of the intellectuals amongst the women, one was a Greek actress who spoke German and recited poetry. Other women composed poems, and told stories to provide a modicum of entertainment. A group of women made plans to go to Israel when the war was over; which they eventually did. Their life before Auschwitz and what would come afterward were constant subjects of dreams, prayers, and daily conversations.

Margot developed gall bladder trouble and received exceptional care from the Polish doctor in the barrack. She was recovering in her bunk while a woman took her place in a work group. All of a sudden, Margot heard someone call, "Is number 47574 here?"

"Yes, that is my number," Margot replied. The guard wanted assurance that Margot was still there. The woman who had replaced her in the work *kommando* had tried to escape. Guards with dogs had searched the territory for the woman. When they found her, she jumped into the river and tried to swim away. She was immediately shot and killed.

Margot and some of the other prisoners witnessed the execution of people in Auschwitz who tried to escape. This was a tactic often used by the Nazis to scare prisoners from escape attempts. Next door, Block 11, was the bunker where they shot and hung condemned prisoners. During the short time the inmates spent there, they were treated far worse than they were previously. They heard many doomed inmates voice their strong convictions before perishing. Some made political exclamations, shouts for justice and prayers. Most inmates sent to Block 11 did not survive.

A woman from a German brothel was once brought to Block 10. She had fallen ill and was placed directly into one of the downstairs' sick rooms. This woman must have been very important, because she received special treatment during her stay. One of the nurses, Marie Hertsdal, was designated to care for her. Margot considered Marie to be her "camp mother," an older person whom she had met in Holland. They had been associated through business with Lo's parents. Marie told Margot about the German woman, but not the entire story. Care was taken to keep this very secretive. Margot does not remember what eventually happened to the woman from Germany.

Toward the end of Margot's stay in Block 10, there was a German guard assigned to work there. His mother came to Auschwitz to visit him. That was the first time this woman witnessed what really took place in the concentration camp. Prior to her arrival there, she did not know. She only considered the Germans who suffered from the destruction of the war. She was shocked by what she saw at Auschwitz. Due to the system of rewards and threats developed by the Nazis, it was difficult to know who could safely be trusted. Therefore, very little information leaked to the public. Nazis were very clandestine. They took extreme care to keep the truth from being known.

The Nazis also went to great lengths to deceive the victims of their ultimate destinations. The suitcase which each deportee was required to take from home was never seen by them again, even if they were chosen to be kept alive. The clothing and the valuables taken from them were sorted in "Canada." Many of the goods were sent to German cities after they had been bombed. The recipient citizens were told that these items were "gifts of love" from their allies.

There were times, such as when thousands of Hungarian Jews were transported to Auschwitz in 1944,

when there were too many people arriving and the burning
process could not keep up. The Nazis dug huge trenches
in the woods into which they dumped thousands of
corpses, poured petroleum on them, and set them afire.
Sometimes living children and adults were thrown into
the flaming trenches and they died a horrible death by fire.
The distinctive, burning smell which permeated the air of
Auschwitz became even stronger.

Survival at Auschwitz was sheer chance; some
people were fortunate. The instinct and will to survive
cannot be discounted. Margot was determined and hopeful.
The reasons for this resolve were many and varied. The
chances for survival were usually greater for prisoners
who had this determination. They were more likely to take
advantage of opportunities that would facilitate survival.
They were pragmatic risk takers – they tried to stay cleaner,
to ward off disease, went to greater lengths to procure
food; forged connections with those who might prove to be
useful, etc.

When Margot was led through the gate at Auschwitz
in April, 1943, she felt sure she would survive but that Lo
would not. She knew she would someday leave - alone.
Never in her life was she so convinced of anything. She
thinks this belief must have been apparent to others,
because she was often told that she never had the downcast,
defeated look prisoners so often acquired. She always
looked everyone straight in the face.

My will to Live. . .

SLW: What was the hardest part of your imprisonment at Auschwitz?

RMD: I always felt like the hardest thing was the uncertainty of what, when, where. If you are a prisoner someplace and you get a sentence, you know how much time you have left to serve and you might have a chance to come out earlier with good behavior. In this case, you didn't know anything. That was actually the most distressing part of the whole experience, where people got the most disheartened. Because you didn't know what was hanging over your head.

CLM: Before being sent to Auschwitz, you were a "light smoker, a social smoker." What was your experience like in camp, regarding smoking?

RMD: Once I gave my portion of bread for one cigarette. Not a pack, just one. I was sitting at what used to be the window, which was gated with plywood, and I was sitting on that window sill smoking that cigarette. It took away my desire for cigarettes because I didn't feel good, I got very dizzy.

CLM: While you were in Auschwitz, did you ever feel panic, like you wouldn't make it?

RMD: No. Again, my fatalism. What was meant to happen was going to happen. Who am I to go against it?

SLW: On a normal day, would you just wait for direction to do something? Was there a routine?

RMD: The routine was you got woken up in the morning, and I guess it was about 5:00, with a lot of yelling and screaming by the earlier arrivals who already had positions. And for the best of myself, if you would offer me a fortune, I cannot remember how we managed with that one little bathroom for all the people. It was not even a bathroom, but more like a stable with a drinking trough. It had a basin with single faucets. The water was not drinkable. That was one of the first things that went around when I arrived at Auschwitz – "Don't drink the water." And ever since that time, I have not relearned to drink great amounts of fluids.

CLM: Did you ever have anything to read in Auschwitz?

RMD: No. You talked. You had a group of people, and I was in a group too, who had a little bit of intellectual exchange. The lower the spiritual state of the person, the more they had to exaggerate. It was something normal. I always say there were a lot of Dutch trades people from the day markets, ones who went around to collect used clothes and whatever, and the daughters of this group of people. If they could have had gold plates, they would have eaten from gold plates. They highly exaggerated.

Dear Mrs. DeWilde,
Thank you for taking the time to tell us about your Holocaust experience. I thought it was very interesting that you still have your number on your arm. I know that it takes courage to tell a large group of people horrible things that you've seen. It sounds horrible that you had to witness people getting hung and that you lost your husband. Thank you for sharing your story.

Jon

Dear Mrs. DeWilde,
Thank you so much for coming to talk to us. One specific point in your story that struck me was that you had to witness a hanging. Also, another thing that I thought was interesting was that there was a prison within the camp.

Always,
Shelagh

Dear Mrs. DeWilde,

Your story really opened my eyes to how the Holocaust affected the lives of people. It's one thing to read a book or see a movie, but listening to you tell your story really struck something in me. I was very sad and sorry that your husband didn't make it through to be with you. I'm sure his soul has moved on to another person or very beautiful thing of nature. Thank you very much for coming.

Sincerely,
Gavin

Margot DeWilde,

Thank you for coming to tell us about the Holocaust. I like how you gave "stealing" a new word in the camp. I also like how you picked and ate the good mushrooms and gave the German officers the bad, big mushrooms. While you were speaking, I felt like I was in the camp.

Thanks,
Nick

Chapter 9
The Death March

By 1943, up to 15,000 prisoners were being killed
each day at Auschwitz. (6, pg. 141) As much as the Nazis
tried to conceal the truth about what was actually taking
place at Auschwitz and other concentration camps, some
information leaked and reached the outside world. Jewish
leaders began urging the Allies to bomb the camp in order
to at least bring a temporary halt to the killings. The Allies
refused, claiming they needed their planes for bombing
military targets. U.S. bombers dropped bombs nearby,
though, aiming for the synthetic-oil plant affiliated with
Auschwitz. (3, pg. 74)

Margot stayed in Block 10 in Auschwitz until
September, 1944. The building was then emptied and the
prisoners were sent to a lone barrack outside the guarded
fence of Auschwitz which housed a sewing *kommando*.
There were picnic benches in the attic where the women
worked long hours repairing used clothing.

One day, Margot sat at one of the picnic tables
with a Dutch friend. She was near the slanted roof of the
barrack and began to feel cramped. Margot said, "Move
over a little, I'm uncomfortable." Her friend moved over
so that Margot could slide away from the slanted ceiling.
A moment later a rock crashed through the roof and landed
right on the spot where Margot had been sitting.

The Allied troops had dropped an explosive in that
area. They were told to avoid bombing the area because

prisoners were working there. On this day, they dropped their ordinance close to a nearby factory. The explosion caused some debris to go flying into the air, some of which tore through the roof of the building where Margot was working. At that ensuing moment of panic, the women who were upstairs directly under the roof tried to dash downstairs, and those who were downstairs tried to go upstairs.

The doors of the barrack were left open by the German guards who had fled into bunkers in the cellar. Some of the prisoners ran outside and could have attempted escape, since the guards were gone. There was a diabetic inmate who was rather corpulent. Not seeing the doors open, she tried to squeeze through the bars of the window and became stuck. She had to be wrenched out later by being pulled backward. Thoughts of escape among the majority of the women were quelled by the thought that they did not know where they could go that would be safe enough to be worth the risk of death. It was no use; the Germans soon herded everybody back into the barrack and life continued as before.

During this time, the early fall of 1944, Himmler finally decided to stop the gassings at Auschwitz. Hoess had already relinquished his command of the camp to Richard Baer on July 29th. The Nazi regime had, by now, begun to crumble. Thousands of people were still being transported to Auschwitz, yet many were also being shipped back to Germany to toil in armament factories. On October 28, a group of 1,700 Jews arrived from Theresienstadt, a walled military town in Czechoslovakia that had become a concentration camp. They were put to death, marking them as the last of the victims of Zyklon B.

Prisoners still faced summary executions, starvation and dysentery, but the mass slaughter had finally ended. On November 26, an order given by Himmler stated: "The crematoria at Auschwitz are to be dismantled..." Groups of prisoners began taking apart the crematoria, but one was kept burning in order to obliterate incriminating papers and deal with "routine" deaths. (3, pgs. 77-78)

Allied troops began approaching concentration camps in the east and west by early 1945. The Nazis scrambled to move prisoners to central camps such as Ravensbruck, Mauthausen, Dachau and Belsen, and to hide and destroy evidence of their reprehensible deeds. The days of the death marches began. The Nazis abandoned Auschwitz on January 18, 1945, leaving behind the prisoners whom they considered too old or weak to travel to another camp. They led over 50,000 prisoners on a forced westward march.

For Margot, this arduous journey began after she had been working in the sewing *kommando* for a few months. On January 18, 1945, she and the other women in her group were ordered to stand outside in rows for a counting session. Although each prisoner was issued a coat, it was extremely cold. Margot heard one of her Dutch acquaintances, Ann Vrachtdoender, ask, "Margot, don't you have a loaf of bread?"

She replied, "No, I didn't notice." Loaves of bread had been distributed, but Margot was not present at the time. That night, after the counting, they were ordered to begin walking. The railroad in that area had been bombed so they were unable to travel by train. They walked for three days and two nights, travelling approximately 60 miles. The prisoners suffered horribly in the bitter cold.

They were surrounded by armed guards with dogs. Many of the prisoners reached the limit of their endurance and fell down in the snow. They soon died of exposure, were shot by the guards or caught by the dogs. Some of the women felt that dying in the cold snow was a graceful, peaceful way to die, and it happened quickly.

They did their best to support and help each other when they could not find the strength to continue by themselves. Ann, along with another friend, named Laura, joined with Margot during the march. Together, they aided Margot because she had cared for them when they were in the hospital room with scarlet fever. She had nothing to eat except the few bites of bread the women shared with her. The prisoners were given no water; they ate snow. Margot remembers only one time being allowed to lean against a building for a short rest.

The long march finally concluded at the next railway station, where open boxcars were waiting for the prisoners. Some had their food bowls they had carried with them, and some still had part of a loaf of bread. With these two exceptions, they were destitute of possessions. The prisoners were ordered into the train. Some of the open boxcars were already filled with people from other camps who had also been forced to march to the station.

The train departed and headed west, away from the Russian troops who were rapidly advancing. The Nazis, having caused great destruction in Russia, were afraid of retaliation. Meanwhile, in Auschwitz, the prisoners left behind had no food or water. Many died from starvation and disease. On January 27, 1945, just days after being abandoned, Soviet troops arrived and liberated the prisoners. There were approximately 7000 inmates still alive. (2, pg. 591)

Along with the other prisoners who had survived the death march, Margot travelled by train to an unknown destination. There were no lavatory facilities or even a bucket to use, so they utilized one of their food bowls. The prisoners were in a boxcar with an open roof, so Margot threw out the contents of the bowl. There happened to be a man walking between the boxcars. He responded with loud cursing, but was unable to retaliate. This inadvertent act of defiance supported Margot and the others and helped them through that cold, miserable train ride.

The prisoners finally concluded their journey to Ravensbruck. This was a political women's concentration camp, fifty miles north of Berlin. It was a destination for prisoners evacuated from camps in the east. Of all the concentration camps in Germany, this one had an extremely high percentage of executed prisoners. When Margot arrived at this camp, thousands of people were being gassed in the camp's final months. Margot did not go through another *selektion*, but was kept alive with the women who arrived with her from Auschwitz. She was assigned a new number and became prisoner 103657. This number was stamped on a metal tag which she was ordered to wear.

Leaving Auschwitz. . .

CLM: Did any news of the war ever reach you during your imprisonment?

RMD: Yes, sometimes. I remember one time when Hoess had fled to England and I remember that someone was sweeping the floor and saying, "Hoess, England, Hoess, England" as they were sweeping. And sometimes you got a little bit of news about the attack on Hitler, the one that was in the office. But for the rest, I don't think we got much news. The big things, we learned later about - after liberation.

SLW: Were you any healthier than the average prisoner on the death march because of your assignment to the medical block?

RMD: Yes, I was in better shape. I must have had a very healthy structure. And those of us in Block 10 were "bought material" – they did not set out to kill us so we were treated a little better and therefore we were a little stronger when it came time to walk away.

Dear Mrs. DeWilde,

I appreciated you taking the time to come speak to us. You endured a lot and are still a strong spirited person. Your story was very moving. It was a great experience for me to hear first-hand what we have studied. The thing that struck me the most was that throughout all the death and hardship you saw and experienced, you seemed to stay strong throughout all of it. I admire your courage. Thank you for coming to speak.

John

Dear Margot,

Your presentation of your experiences in the concentration camps was astounding. Your descriptions of the horrible events that took place made the Holocaust come more alive and real. You didn't focus on the bad things, but more the good. The mushrooms, the blankets, and everything else you said made it very enjoyable. Thank you very much.

Sincerely,
Brandon

Chapter 10
The Three Musketeers

Margot, along with her friends (Ann and Laura) who survived the death march, were at Ravensbruck for only three days. They remained together constantly and became known as the Three Musketeers. The first time a call went out for volunteers to go on a transport, all three volunteered. The three were taken away in trucks along with other inmate volunteers. This act may have saved Margot's and her friends' lives. Many of the other prisoners who arrived at Ravensbruck were sent immediately to their deaths. (2)

The volunteers arrived at a civilian labor camp near Malchow. Women who did not want to work for the Germans were taken to that camp and put to work. Not only Jews, but various other political prisoners were in the highly crowded labor camp. When they arrived, no more bunks were available, so they slept on a layer of straw on the floor, "practically like sardines in a can." They were packed together so tightly that when night came, it was best not to leave one's spot, as it would most likely be taken.

Laura remained at the camp while Margot and Ann were sent to labor. Margot was assigned to work in a factory nearby which produced cardboard boxes for ammunition. It was run by a couple who had arrived from Leipzig, Germany, after fleeing from the Russians. However, they also paid the Germans to have additional prisoners labor for them. French prisoners were doing most of the labor in the factory.

Ann was working in a civilian kitchen, which was
next door to the cardboard factory. When the couple from
Leipzig learned that some of their laborers arrived from
a concentration camp, they immediately ordered soup for
them. They sympathized with Margot, Ann and the others
because they had heard of the terrible conditions at the
camps and it was visibly obvious that these women had not
been receiving enough food. The soup they were given
was much more substantial than the watery broth they were
used to. This extra nourishment greatly helped to restore
them.

The workers in the factory and the kitchen shared
an outhouse. At a certain time of day, Ann would go to the
outhouse and on the way knock on a wall of the cardboard
factory. Margot would hear her knock, and then also obtain
permission to use the lavatory. There they would meet,
and Ann would transfer some edibles she had stolen from
the kitchen to Margot. Margot hid the food in the lining
of her coat. At night, when they marched back to camp,
some of the inmates were searched. The prisoners from
the cardboard factory did not get checked, but those from
the civilian kitchen were almost always frisked. So Margot
marched out of the manufacturing plant back into the
camp with the hidden food, and took it into their barrack.
This extra food helped them to regain some strength.
Eventually, though, suspicion was raised and they were
relieved from their "jobs."

Margot and the other prisoners from the barrack
were marched outside in the cold every day for counting.
Without adequate clothing many injuries resulted from this
inhumane treatment. One night after the counting session,

Margot stood but could not walk. She discovered that her feet were frostbitten and covered with enormous blisters. Margot somehow obtained a pin and a paper bandage. She drained the blisters and bandaged her feet with the paper. Except for some visible scars, she suffered relatively little damage to her feet. Some people had toes or feet amputated because of damage from the cold. But thanks to her relatively healthy constitution, she was able to avoid such extremes.

Because of crowded and unsanitary conditions, along with nothing but straw for bedding, hygiene became a problem. Margot and her friends were finally infested with lice. They had managed to avoid infestation during their imprisonment at Auschwitz. Their hair had not been cut since they first arrived in Auschwitz. After that haircut they kept their heads covered with scarves. By the time they arrived at Malchow, their hair had grown longer which increased their chances of becoming infested. They picked the lice from each other's heads to stay a little cleaner and to help the itching.

Margot does not remember much of her time at this camp near Malchow or what she did from one day to the next after being relieved from duty at the factory. For most of the remainder of her time at this labor camp, she was confined to the barrack.

Discussing philosophy. . .

CLM: You seem devoid of anger. As a prisoner were you angry?

RMD: No. I believe that things come the way they have to come and I never have had hatred. Of course, I regret the whole war. It is a hard way to learn to appreciate life! And there were some frustrations, of course.

SLW: How do you feel toward Germans now?

RMD: I admire them for having perked up again, which was thanks to the Marshall Plan. But I don't have any bad feelings about it and I feel that if there are still some Nazis alive today, which would be as old as Methuselah, they must have had a lot of thinking to do. And if they haven't changed in that period, it doesn't matter. Because only activity makes changes, not if you get along and say no, we were the best and we did this and we did that because it was the best thing to do. Like most people would say, yeah, we made our mistakes in that time and now we have matters different. But there are some who didn't. They have ruined their own lives. They don't see what they did as horrendous, because they were told to do so. They were following orders. If they could have convinced the Nazis of something different, it wouldn't have happened.

Dear Margot DeWilde,
You had so much faith and you were so brave.
You taught me things I never knew before.
Thank you so much. You made me think and
have hope and be brave. Your talking to us
helped me see the truth of life and to take one
day at a time and always be there for each other.

Love,
Grace

Margot,
It is really a once in a lifetime chance to hear
from a survivor like yourself. Thanks for giving
all of us the opportunity. Your story is truly an
amazing story of courage. You are one of the
strongest people I've ever met. Thank you again.
I am so lucky to have heard your life story.

Always,
Charlotte

Chapter 11
Liberation and Reunions

During Margot's imprisonment in the labor camp near Malchow, the prisoners often heard the sounds of shootings and sirens. There was commotion in the distance. Margot and her friends deduced that they were near the front line. This camp was not as secluded as Auschwitz. Some of the prisoners gathered together to discuss the possibility of liberation. They felt the end of the war must be approaching and speculated who might arrive to release them. They decided someone should be designated to communicate with the troops. As Margot had picked up some English over the years, she volunteered to communicate with any English-speaking troops. A Polish inmate who spoke some Russian volunteered to speak with any Russians who might arrive.

The prisoners waited day after day, increasingly hopeful that liberators would arrive soon. One night, Margot and the Polish woman decided to stay awake all night. They reasoned that when they were liberated, they wanted to make the soldiers understand who they were.

Nothing happened during that night, but the next morning the prisoners were not awakened by the German guards, with the usual cursing and yelling. Margot and the other woman were still awake, while everyone else was asleep on the straw. Margot peered through a window and saw a man wearing a blue and white striped prison uniform, walking in the distance and carrying an American flag. She felt she must be hallucinating and decided not to alert the other prisoners. She did not dare call anyone else to look, because she thought it was simply wishful thinking that was clouding her mind. That was the last week in April, 1945.

Finally, a male prisoner came into the building and woke the sleeping women by telling them they should get up. They were liberated. A short while later, another prisoner said to the women, "Get out of here! You're free!" He explained that the Russians were coming from the east, so they should head westward toward their allies. It was surprising to Margot to be liberated in such an unofficial manner. After the initial shock, she had an intense feeling of joy such as she had never felt before!

Ann, Laura and Margot did not have any possessions to gather other than their food bowls, so they began walking immediately. They joined the march with hundreds of German civilians heading west, who were carrying packages of various sizes. The citizens pushed buggies filled with furniture and other possessions. They knew the Russians would be arriving soon, and they wanted to get away from them in time. Many guards and the SS had put on civilian clothing, in the hopes of avoiding detection by the Russians. They were afraid that the Russians might retaliate because of the atrocities they had committed in Russia and Poland. Some escaped eventual retribution, but many of the German SS were caught because of their underarm tattoos.

The Three Musketeers began another long march together. Their feelings were indescribable as they now travelled in freedom. The weather was warmer, so they did not have to contend with the bitter cold. There were no guards to drive them on with constant threats of death; they could stop and rest whenever they desired. Occasionally, they saw a group of prisoners who had stolen some food, such as potatoes, from farms and had made fires to roast the food. They were usually willing to share, so Margot and her friends were given portions.

That night, nearing the end of their first day of freedom, Margot, Ann and Laura searched for a place to spend the night. They stopped at a farm and sneaked into the chicken coop. It had a ladder leading to a loft where they fell asleep in the hay, exhausted and hungry, yet peaceful. They woke the next morning famished, but had nothing to eat. Ann said she would go look for some food. Before long, she came back with a little suckling pig under her arm. "Here is something to eat!" she said.

Margot looked at her in disbelief and said, "What do you think we can do with that thing?! That's a baby! That's a live animal! Who do you think is going to slaughter it? Nobody. Take it back to the farm!" The farm woman had looked angrily at Ann when she took the piglet. With the great numbers who had been recently travelling through the area, German civilians had become accustomed to former prisoners passing through their farms and stealing food. Many other released prisoners would have taken more, but Margot and her friends did not feel they should do this. Nor could they kill a living creature, so the piglet was released.

Next they captured a chicken, which they decided to hold hostage until it laid an egg because they could not kill the chicken, either. After a short wait, the chicken deposited an egg and was released. They broke the egg into one of their food bowls, added some water to it and drank.

"Immediately, we became sick and heaved the egg back up!" recalls Margot. But since they did not have anything else in their stomachs, their nausea did not last long.

In the afternoon, they began walking west again. They soon found that the Russians circled the German troops and arrived at the next town before they did. Margot and her friends were interrogated by Russian officers, who treated them very courteously. The women were able to prove that they were prisoners not only by the tattooed numbers on their arms, but also because of their emaciated conditions.

One of the Russian officers approached Margot and her friends with a Dutch-Russian dictionary, after hearing that they were from Holland. Before the war, he had learned that sometime during the 1400's, Russian Tsar Peter was sent when he was young to Holland to learn ship building. He was fascinated by this history and since then had always wanted to visit Holland. Thus, he carried the dictionary in case he visited Holland, to help him communicate in Dutch. He used it for a short time to communicate with Margot.

The Russians treated Margot and her friends very well. The women were given a loaf of bread to share. They were housed in a private home that German civilians had been forced to vacate. This house, along with all the others in town, did not have running water. They had to walk to a small lake to carry enough water for their use. Compared to their lack of water in the prisons, though, this was a luxury. They had a roof over their heads and each had a bed with blankets and sheets. The house had cabinets which they spent time looking through. Margot found Dutch cocoa powder which she used to make hot chocolate!

The first day they spent in the house, they took the opportunity to bathe themselves. Laura was busy washing herself when a Russian soldier brought them more bread. She startled him, speaking very loudly. He could not understand her, as she was yelling in Dutch for him to leave. He set the bread on the table and quickly departed.

On the second day, they heard there was a Red Cross post nearby. It was across a heather field, which was burning. Margot does not remember how they managed to cross the smoldering field, but eventually they arrived at the post. They found that it was a French Red Cross post. Again, the three musketeers were taken in and cared for. From there, they were transported by truck from one small collection camp to another. The Red Cross was not prepared to find so many released prisoners, but did their best to accommodate them. The liberated prisoners slept in tents and barracks during their stops. They travelled through Germany over a span of six days, escorted by Canadian soldiers, and finally arrived in the southern part of Holland.

Margot and her friends were sprayed with DDT. After they received clean clothing and were checked medically, they were told that they had to wait a while until they could return to northern Holland. Since Amsterdam was liberated about six months after southern Holland, Dutch citizens in the south had to be supplied with food first. They did not have a food distribution system in place so the northern region did not allow liberated prisoners and citizens to return from the south.

Next, they travelled to another holding camp near Amersfoord. This camp was used during wartime as a prison run by the Gestapo. They imprisoned and killed countless people there. After liberation, it was turned into a temporary holding camp for returning Dutch prisoners.

From there, Margot, Ann and Laura were sent to Enschede. They were housed in a school that had become a temporary holding camp. There was a priest who visited there and Margot spoke with him. He told her she could write a letter to whomever she wanted and he would mail it. She wrote a letter to the in-between address in Amsterdam. In the letter, Margot notified her father of her location and informed him that she was well.

Margot also requested that the priest investigate if a business relation of Alex Meyer's, who had a textile manufacturing factory in the area, was still living in Enschede. A short time later he returned with the news that he had found the business acquaintance and his family. They wanted Margot to come to their house right away. Margot turned down this invitation, because she had been through so much with her two friends and did want to leave them. She asked the priest to thank the family for her and give her regards. However, the priest said that he had already been told that Margot's friends were also invited to the home. This caused Margot to change her mind and accept the invitation.

The Three Musketeers were received by the family and treated exceptionally well. Soon after arriving, their hostess suggested they have a garden party, because of the beautiful weather in May, 1945. She invited the Canadian soldiers who had escorted them from camp to camp on their way back to Holland. They were all sitting outside together, when suddenly another Canadian soldier appeared. Margot's hostess asked her, "Is this an acquaintance of yours, too?"

"No," Margot said, "the only soldiers I know are sitting here." The man spoke briefly with her hostess, then turned around and approached Margot. Margot was shocked to realize this man was her brother, Manfred! He had come out of hiding along with their mother half a year earlier when Arnhem was liberated. Manfred had then joined the Canadian Army as an interpreter. He was now called Peter because it was the name he had taken when he went into hiding and it was the name which he printed on his false papers. He was in uniform, had been given a pass and went searching for Margot. He was able to find her because he was with his father when the priest delivered the letter from Margot. His father was in the same building as the Danish woman. From her brother, Margot learned that their parents had also survived the war. Peter gave Margot ten guilders and some clothing their mother had kept hidden for her. Margot's brother, who kept the name Peter for the rest of his life, stayed with Margot for a short time before returning to his military duty. Margot and her companions stayed for a week with the family in Enschede.

All train stations in the area had been temporarily shut down. Eventually, the trains began to transport passengers again. Margot, along with Ann and Laura, took the first train to Amsterdam. Upon arrival, the three friends finally separated. With promises to stay in touch, each set off on foot to different addresses. Margot travelled to the address of the Danish lady to whom Margot had sent letters to her father throughout the war. It was across the street from where her uncle used to live and where her family resided when they moved to Holland. It was about a half hour walk from the railway station. When Margot arrived there, she was finally reunited with her father and brother.

Her mother was still in Arnhem where she had been in hiding.

After a few days, Margot's mother returned to Amsterdam. The family temporarily resided at a bed and breakfast. Her parents had a room and Margot rented her own room. After his discharge from the service, Peter joined them. They stayed there until other housing was available. Holland had lost numerous buildings throughout the war; they were demolished and scavenged for materials. During the rebuilding phase, many families were not able to find an apartment.

Thus Margot began her new life after the war. She survived imprisonment for over two years. She now had a soft bed to sleep on and a room of her own. Her appetite seemed insatiable! She constantly ate in order to regain the weight she had lost. Like so many other liberated prisoners, Margot stashed a supply of food. She kept a box of square k-ration cookies under her bed in order to always have something available to eat.

All for One. . .

SLW: To what do you attribute your survival?

RMD: I always claimed, which was very un-Jewish,
that I had a guardian angel. The guardian angel is
your unconsciousness, something you cannot
explain, but we all have it. And if you follow that
idea, then it turns out okay. If I started thinking
logically and went against it, things went wrong.

Throughout all my ordeals, I always seemed
to meet people who helped me. If I would have
known ahead of time what was going to happen, I
would have never thought I could have survived.
I learned that however bad a situation you are in,
you can survive. If you have the will to survive,
to live, to establish something, anybody can live
through anything. Nothing is impossible if you
really work at it. Anything is possible. Somehow,
I knew I would survive when I arrived at
Auschwitz. I knew I would come out alone.
Somehow, I knew my husband wouldn't make it.

As a child, I already was what my parents
called a *daffkeponem*. In my looks, my posture, I
was what my parents would consider someone who
always goes against everything that she's supposed
to do. And in this case, I was not about to be killed.
I would try to do the utmost to stay alive, not
because life was so valuable, but I did not want to
give in, to be destroyed by a power which thought it
was stronger than I was.

CLM: Did you remain friends with Ann & Laura after the war?

RMD: Yes, we kept in touch for many years, even after I moved to the United States.

CLM: Do you have a philosophy gained from your experiences at Auschwitz that you would like to share with others?

RMD: I think there is a need to connect with the past. Because from every move, from every action and reaction, you inherit something. I have come to the conclusion that Judaism is not a race, it's a philosophy passed on from generation to generation, enclosed in the experiences of those generations. And you can't run away from it. I'm not religious, yet I am aware of every holiday that comes around. I don't believe in resurrection, whether it be Jewish or Christian, when the Messiah comes. I believe that the soul of a person lives forever. I try to connect with as many souls as I can. I believe that the souls of people stay alive and that your actions in your lifetime determine the placement of that soul into what you have earned by your behavior.

... I'm glad to hear after you were freed you didn't take life for granted. You went out and lived and didn't let this horrific event hold you back. You are an inspiration to not let anything hold me back in life. And to just keep pushing forward. You truly are such a strong woman and I am so sorry that this happened to you, but I am glad you were one of the survivors. Thanks again for coming and sharing.

Keep living,
Carolyn

Dear Margot DeWilde,
Thank you so much for coming to talk to us! You were a great speaker! I thought it was very interesting that you were there for exactly 2 years, 2 months, and 2 days.

Thanks again!
Michelle

Dear Margot DeWilde,
Thank you so much for coming and speaking to us. It was so interesting to hear your story. I found it to be an amazing experience. It was wonderful to learn that your brother survived the war. I really enjoyed your story. Thank you so much again.

Respectfully,
Tom

Dear Mrs. DeWilde,
Thank you so much for coming in and talking about your life. It was interesting to listen to your story about the Holocaust. It was funny to listen to what you thought about after you were liberated, the fact that you just wanted to make up for the time wasted. I just want to thank you again.

Sheila

Chapter 12
Life after the War

On the first anniversary of the liberation of Auschwitz, in early 1946, a party was held in Amsterdam which Margot attended. She met a young man there named Rein Woltz who had returned to Holland in August. He had been a prisoner in a camp in Indonesia. During the war, he was a cook on a merchant ship. When the ship was hit by a torpedo in 1942, he was taken prisoner of war by the Japanese. He and Margot quickly became romantically involved and decided to marry. Although they could not legally marry at this time, he lived in with Margot at the Bed and Breakfast. According to Dutch law, Margot had to wait over five years before Lo was officially declared dead because she was not issued his death certificate.

Margot finally remarried in 1951 and found an apartment with her new husband. They had an architect remodel the living space, tearing down and rebuilding the walls and adding central heat. Here they lived happily together for many years.

Her husband, Rein, bought a record and radio store with money Margot had inherited from Lo's share of his parent's fortune. A woman named Tine, who had managed the store, continued to help run the business. She became part of their family, living in a room upstairs. Over the next few years, making more money became Rein's highest priority. After thirteen years together, in 1959, Margot decided to end the relationship by filing for divorce.

Once her divorce was granted, Margot decided to travel in the United States to visit friends and family and see new sites. She arrived in November, 1959, to visit her cousins in New York. Next, she travelled to Richfield, Minnesota, where her brother, Peter, and his family had settled. Then she went to Santa Ana, California, to visit an older couple whom she met in Amsterdam after the war. She had become good friends with them. They had extended an open invitation for Margot to visit them. She stayed two months visiting these "second parents." They travelled together throughout southern California.

Margot then returned to Peter; his wife, Hermiene (Vecht); and their two-year-old baby girl, Patricia. They were expecting their second baby, and Margot thought she could be useful. She arrived in Richfield before the baby was due. By this time, Margot knew she would never be able to have children of her own. She had survived the war, but, because of the sterilization treatment, she was infertile. She had grown very close to her brother. However, with constant talk about babies and Dr. Spock, Margot sometimes felt the need to be alone.

One day she decided to take a bus to downtown Minneapolis. She arrived at the bus stop at the same time as another woman, both just missing the bus. They began talking, and Margot told her of her time in California, where the weather and people were warm. But here in Minnesota, the weather was cold and the people seemed cold, too. In an attempt to be friendly, the woman told Margot about a Dutch family whom she knew. The woman later contacted the family who then invited Margot to dinner and a meeting of the Dutch club. Margot accepted the invitation and went to the family's house. After dinner she began talking to Rudy DeWilde, the oldest of four sons. They visited for several hours and missed the meeting! Rudy and Margot quickly became good friends.

He told her about his life during the war. Rudy was in the Dutch Air Force stationed in Indonesia. In 1948, Indonesia became independent from the Netherlands. He was one of the last Dutch soldiers to leave Indonesia. When he returned home, jobs were very scarce. The government offered relocation expenses to young people who volunteered to leave the country. They were asked to move to other countries, such as the United States, Canada, and Australia. He first moved to Australia and found a job as a cook in a children's hospital. After his parents immigrated to the United States in the mid-1950s, they applied for a visa for Rudy. They were given help from a lawyer where his mother was working. The lawyer knew Senator Hubert Humphrey, who facilitated the swift procurement of Rudy's visa. A week after he arrived in the United States, in 1956, he landed a job at a grocery store called Red Owl.

Margot helped after the birth of Peter and Hermiene's second baby, in March, 1960. She enjoyed this new life caring for the children. Peter and Hermiene lovingly designated Margot as a third parent to their children. She was scheduled to leave the country soon, because her visa was about to expire. Margot promised Rudy she would come back to Minnesota.

Margot decided she would like to make a permanent move to America. When she returned to Holland, she applied for immigration. She sold some of her personal belongings, gave some to her parents, and the rest were shipped to Minnesota. Before she left Amsterdam on

January 2, 1961, she promised her parents that she would visit as often as she could, feeling that Peter had deserted them already. In March, 1961, soon after arriving back in Richfield, Margot and Rudy were married.

A few months after the marriage, Rudy quit working at Red Owl. He and Margot travelled to Holland that fall. When they returned to the United States in 1962, they opened a coffee shop called "The Loeb Arcade Luncheonette" on Hennepin Avenue in downtown Minneapolis. It was near Northern States Power Company headquarters. Many employees came in for breakfast or lunch and a ten cent cup of coffee (with free refills). The coffee shop remained open for three and a half years.

After that, Margot and Rudy travelled for half a year. Then Rudy began searching for employment. He met Mr. Lund, who was impressed with his cooking and produce expertise. Regardless of not needing another employee at the time, he hired Rudy to work at his grocery store on Lake Street in Minneapolis.

Rudy worked in the produce department at Lund's for twenty-five years. He and Margot remained married for forty-four years. Rudy was seven years younger than Margot. She often joked that she married a younger man so she could be taken care of when she grew old. Unfortunately, though, he died on April 7, 2005, of congestive heart failure. Margot scattered Rudy's ashes on Lake Mille Lacs in Minnesota, his favorite spot where they had a cabin for many years.

Margot has spoken to hundreds of audiences since 1969. She shares the experiences of her imprisonment. Many of her talks are given at schools, thereby educating and influencing many young people. She feels it is her duty

to continue talking as long as she is able. She has inspired
countless individuals with her remarkable capacity for
forgiveness and ability to see purpose and meaning in life
when faced with the unimaginable.

[Note: Margot has never accepted payment for speaking.
Honorariums are donated to the Jewish Community
Relations Council of Minnesota and the Dakotas. It is
the program that runs the speakers Bureau; Tolerance
Minnesota.]

Mother, Father, Brother. . .

SLW: How did your parents feel about you and Peter moving so far away?

RMD: They were very sad about it, but because they thought it was best for us, they accepted it.

SLW: How often did you return to the Netherlands to visit your parents after moving to America?

RMD: Every one and a half to two years. My father passed away on November 3, 1967. I returned to Holland and was there at his death. I had been there earlier in the year for a visit. He became ill after I left, so I returned. After his death, my mother travelled with me back to the United States. She was suffering from some dementia and could not acclimate to life in the U.S. Peter had put her name on a list to go into an assisted living home in Holland when he returned to Holland for the first time after the war. She was in the U.S. from November, 1967 to June, 1968. When there was an opening for her at the home, she returned to Holland. She died in July, 1969.

CLM: Did it bother Rudy that you could not have children?

RMD: No, he didn't want children because he had raised his younger brothers. He had three younger brothers who were born 14 years after he was born, so he was the nursemaid. They hated him because he had to order them around, but it was his mother that pushed everything off to Rudy. That was not a pleasant situation.

CLM: Why did you never become an American citizen?

RMD: I could not denounce my loyalty for Holland. My brother and my parents had survived there. In 1940 when the Germans invaded Holland, they took our German nationality away. According to the Germans, we were Jewish, it didn't matter what country we came from, and we were unwanted. At that time, we were still German. And then we had to have a passport which was for foreigners.

CLM: Were you ever given back your German citizenship after the war?

RMD: No, we were stateless. I had a nonsectarian passport and I never applied for anything.

SLW: Would you ever like to go back to Holland to live?

RMD: No. Now Holland is so much changed, that I think somebody that has lived someplace else, like me, would never want to go back. I would go back only for the memories, but not to live, because there's crime and misery and drugs, mostly, it's no fun anymore. It was nice, I have nice memories, good times. Bad memories, too, but that is life. But I always felt like a stranger in paradise. It was my town, my area where I grew up for many years, but still it was like I was in any other city. I didn't see a familiar face, nothing, and you looked for that all the time.

SLW: After the war, when everybody was coming back home, did life become normal quickly?

RMD: For me it did because I had money whereas many people didn't. And I could do things to catch up, and I had extra coupons for having returned from camp that I could use. So I had a fairly good life right after the war, but many people were forced to struggle. So I always say I was different than the average person, by being financially a little more independent. But it wasn't normal for most people. Holland had been plundered. It had no facilities, no exposure to world happenings, they were completely isolated. Everybody had suffered. Coming back to normal life was already a big thing. The Marshall Plan helped financially to get people to be productive again. But for everything to get going again, it took time. And at that time, there was still a lot of unemployment because production wasn't up. And that was a time when they paid young people to go someplace else, to Canada or Australia. They paid part of the passage to get rid of them. And then when so many men were gone, they didn't have any laborers left. We had to bring people in from other countries to rebuild. The Moroccans came first, then workers from eastern countries who were willing to work for low wages and do the handiwork.

CLM: Do you feel that your philosophy has changed over the years, from the time of your liberation to the present?

RMD: Yes. My thinking has changed completely. I was not spiteful after the liberation, but I felt sorry for myself in the beginning. I could not have children, which was difficult for me to accept. I did not have a profession, I did not have any diplomas, and I always felt minor in some way. I felt different, a certain shortcoming within myself. Somehow those feelings developed into something completely different over the years, as I found my true self; found the unknown reason why I'm living. In later years I found a lot of people who understood what I was talking about. When I first came to the United States in the 1960s, people talked about their kids, houses, and sometimes bragged about money, but nothing from the inside was ever mentioned. And I heard people say something to the effect of, "Don't tell me your troubles, I've got enough of my own." So I had my intellectual discussions with the Jehovah's Witnesses who came to visit. We could dispute things; they tried to convince me and I tried to convince them. Over the course of many years came the answers to questions such as, "What am I? In what part of the universe am I? What is the meaning; what is the purpose of life?"

SLW: Do you feel we all have a purpose in life?

RMD: In my feeling, if you call it the universal nature or God or Christ or whatever, if it didn't have a name which would separate us from each other, then we would agree that there is something greater than ourselves who has the recipe for life. And you

145

get put on this earth. I don't believe in death; I believe in stages of life. And you are put in that stage where you have to find your own way – the destination, the end station is set, but how you get there determines what your next stage will be.

CLM: So do you think that you and the other survivors, among so many millions of people, had future work to do in telling what happened or in fulfilling a purpose of educating people?

RMD: Well, the purpose for it was because it is such an unbelievable story. Sometimes I don't believe myself, what happened. Knowing there are people here in this world who denied it, as long as I am here in this universe, I have to bear witness to it. That is my feeling. I have progressed in my way of thinking, by becoming aware of something which I otherwise automatically accepted. So when I'm thinking about things, I'm not getting mad and I say, "Hey, that must be one of the steps of learning." If you're disappointed, or even happy, that is what life is.

SLW: Do you find joy in sharing your experiences?

RMD: Not really joy. It's not something to be proud of or something which you have accomplished; it is a learning process which I had to go through in order to become me. And I have at times thought, "What would have become of that little Margot Lustig that was born in Berlin if all this wouldn't have happened?" You can't imagine; you can't think about it; you can't think logically what would have happened. That's why I came to the conclusion that it's predetermined how life progresses.

Dear Margot DeWilde,

I am so thankful that I was able to experience your presentation. The thing that I enjoyed the most was being able to put a more personal take on the Holocaust and to be able to think past our history books. I will remember it for many years. Thanks again!

Sincerely,
Takeyah

Dear Margot,

. . . Hearing your story was truly inspiring to me and taught me never to give up. I never knew that you had such a scary story. You are an amazing person and an inspiration to all of us.

Thank you so much,
Kylie